one pot
low-fuss food for busy people

THE AUSTRALIAN
Women's Weekly

CONTENTS

Minimum fuss, maximum flavour; that's the one-pot promise, and that's just how I like home-cooking to be. We've kept the mess to just one cooking dish in this book, adapting old favourites to fit the one-pot bill. Single-dish cooking lends itself to comfort food, like slow-cooked casseroles, but you'll be surprised at the delicious sweet and savoury dishes we've managed to create in just a single dish. Perfect for easy cooking and an even easier clean-up.

Pamela Clark

Food Director

Roasts and casseroles: old favourites that our mums prepared with love. These dishes easily satisfy a crowd and fill the home with the welcoming aroma of slow-cooked food.

TRADITIONAL

irish lamb and barley stew

2 tablespoons olive oil

1kg diced lamb shoulder

1 large brown onion (200g), chopped coarsely

2 medium carrots (240g), chopped coarsely

2 trimmed celery stalks (200g), chopped coarsely

2 cloves garlic, crushed

1 litre (4 cups) chicken stock

2 cups (500ml) water

1 cup (200g) pearl barley

4 sprigs fresh thyme

3 medium potatoes (600g), chopped coarsely

2 cups (160g) finely shredded cabbage

⅓ cup finely chopped fresh flat-leaf parsley

1 Heat half the oil in large saucepan; cook lamb, in batches, until browned.

2 Heat remaining oil in same pan; cook onion, carrot, celery and garlic, stirring, until vegetables soften. Return lamb to pan with stock, the water, barley and thyme; bring to the boil. Reduce heat; simmer, covered, 1 hour, skimming fat from surface occasionally.

3 Add potato; simmer, uncovered, about 20 minutes or until potato is tender. Add cabbage; simmer, uncovered, until cabbage is just tender. Discard thyme.

4 Serve stew sprinkled with parsley.

preparation time 20 minutes

cooking time 1 hour 45 minutes **serves** 6

nutritional count per serving 22.6g total fat
(8.2g saturated fat); 2224kJ (532 cal);
37.4g carbohydrate; 40.4g protein; 8.6g fibre

note Recipe is suitable to freeze at the end of step 2.

chilli and lemon-baked veal rack

1 large kumara (500g), sliced thickly
4 medium potatoes (800g), sliced thickly
1 large brown onion (200g), sliced thickly
2 tablespoons olive oil
1 tablespoon lemon juice
3 cloves garlic, crushed
1.6kg veal rack (8 chops), trimmed
2 cups (140g) stale breadcrumbs
1 tablespoon finely grated lemon rind
1 fresh long red chilli, sliced thinly
1 fresh long red chilli, chopped finely
60g butter, melted

1 Preheat oven to 220°C/200°C fan-forced.
2 Combine kumara, potato, onion, oil, juice and two-thirds of the garlic in large ovenproof dish. Place veal on wire rack over potato mixture in dish.
3 Combine remaining garlic, breadcrumbs, rind, chillies and butter in small bowl. Press breadcrumb mixture over veal.
4 Roast, uncovered, about 40 minutes or until cooked as desired. Stand, covered, 10 minutes before serving.

preparation time 15 minutes
cooking time 40 minutes **serves** 8
nutritional count per serving 15.2g total fat
(5.9g saturated fat); 1852kJ (443 cal);
32.2g carbohydrate; 42g protein; 3.7g fibre
note Recipe is not suitable to freeze.

slow-roasted duck with balsamic-glazed vegetables

4 duck marylands (1.2kg), trimmed
2 teaspoons sea salt
2 medium potatoes (400g), chopped coarsely
2 medium carrots (500g), chopped coarsely
2 medium parsnips (460g), chopped coarsely
¼ cup (60ml) balsamic vinegar
20g butter, melted
½ cup firmly packed fresh flat-leaf parsley leaves
⅓ cup (55g) almond kernels

1 Preheat oven to 180°C/160°C fan-forced.
2 Rub skin of duck with sea salt.
3 Combine vegetables, vinegar and butter in large shallow baking dish; arrange vegetables in single layer. Place duck, skin-side up, on top of vegetables. Roast 1¼ hours. Increase temperature to 220°C/200°C fan-forced, roast about 15 minutes or until duck skin is crisp and vegetables are glazed.
4 Toss parsley and nuts with vegetables in baking dish; serve vegetable mixture topped with duck.

preparation time 20 minutes
cooking time 1 hour 30 minutes **serves** 4
nutritional count per serving 66.3g total fat
(19.5g saturated fat); 3440kJ (823 cal);
27.2g carbohydrate; 26.8g protein; 9g fibre
note Recipe is not suitable to freeze.

tip Khitcherie is a classic Indian rice and lentil dish that was anglicised by the Raj to make an English breakfast staple, kedgeree. However, the inclusion of curry powder, garlic and peas soon found it more happily consumed at lunch or dinner. We've adapted it further, by making it with smoked ocean trout rather than the smoked haddock used by the British.

smoked ocean trout kedgeree

You need to cook about 1¾ cups of white medium-grain rice to get the amount of cooked rice required for this recipe.

2 tablespoons olive oil
1 large brown onion (200g), sliced thinly
1 tablespoon brown sugar
2 tablespoons malt vinegar
4 green onions, cut into 3cm lengths
2 cloves garlic, crushed
2 teaspoons mild curry powder
4 cups (600g) cooked white medium-grain rice
600g smoked ocean trout fillets, skinned, flaked
1 cup (120g) frozen peas
1 tablespoon lemon juice
¼ cup finely chopped fresh flat-leaf parsley
4 hard-boiled eggs, quartered

1 Heat half the oil in large frying pan; cook brown onion, stirring, until soft. Add sugar and vinegar; cook, stirring, about 5 minutes or until onion is browned and caramelised. Transfer to small bowl.
2 Heat remaining oil in same pan; cook green onion, garlic and curry powder, stirring, about 3 minutes or until fragrant.
3 Return caramelised onion to pan with rice, fish, peas and juice; stir until heated through. Remove from heat; stir in parsley. Serve kedgeree topped with boiled egg.
preparation time 10 minutes
cooking time 20 minutes **serves** 4
nutritional count per serving 20.7g total fat
(4.3g saturated fat); 2391kJ (572 cal);
51.3g carbohydrate; 42.1g protein; 4.6g fibre
note Recipe is not suitable to freeze.

pasta, bacon and vegetable soup

2 tablespoons olive oil
1 small brown onion (80g), chopped finely
6 rindless bacon rashers (390g), chopped coarsely
2.5 litres (10 cups) water
1kg bacon bones
2 tablespoons tomato paste
3 medium potatoes (600g), quartered
300g piece pumpkin, chopped coarsely
200g cauliflower, chopped coarsely
2½ cups (200g) finely shredded cabbage
1 medium carrot (120g), chopped coarsely
1 cup (110g) frozen beans
1 large zucchini (150g), chopped coarsely
¾ cup (95g) small pasta shells

1 Heat oil in large saucepan; cook onion and bacon rashers, stirring, until onion softens.
2 Add the water, bacon bones, paste, potato, pumpkin and cauliflower; bring to the boil. Reduce heat; simmer, covered, 45 minutes.
3 Remove and discard bacon bones. Using potato masher, roughly crush vegetables.
4 Add cabbage, carrot, beans, zucchini and pasta; simmer, uncovered, about 10 minutes or until pasta is cooked.

preparation time 25 minutes
cooking time 1 hour **serves** 6
nutritional count per serving 18.5g total fat
(5.3g saturated fat); 1760kJ (421 cal);
32.6g carbohydrate; 27.5g protein; 6.8g fibre
note Recipe is not suitable to freeze.

cauliflower, potato and bean soup

1 tablespoon olive oil
1 medium brown onion (150g), chopped finely
1 litre (4 cups) water
1 litre (4 cups) chicken stock
4 medium potatoes (800g), quartered
500g cauliflower, chopped coarsely
2 tablespoons tomato paste
3 cups (450g) frozen broad beans, peeled
2 eggs, beaten lightly
¼ cup (20g) finely grated parmesan cheese
2 tablespoons finely chopped fresh mint

1 Heat oil in large saucepan; cook onion, stirring, until soft.
2 Add the water, stock, potato, cauliflower and paste; bring to the boil. Reduce heat; simmer, uncovered, about 20 minutes or until vegetables are tender.
3 Remove from heat, add beans, egg and cheese; cover, stand 5 minutes. Serve soup sprinkled with mint.

preparation time 15 minutes
cooking time 30 minutes **serves** 4
nutritional count per serving 10.6g total fat
(3g saturated fat); 1601kJ (383 cal);
42.3g carbohydrate; 21.7g protein; 15.5g fibre
note Recipe is not suitable to freeze.

creamy chicken and vegetable casserole

1kg chicken thigh fillets, cut into 2cm pieces
2 tablespoons plain flour
2 tablespoons olive oil
1 large brown onion (200g), chopped coarsely
1 clove garlic, crushed
2 medium carrots (240g), chopped coarsely
2 medium potatoes (400g), chopped coarsely
2 trimmed celery stalks (200g), chopped coarsely
1 cup (250ml) dry white wine
1½ cups (375ml) chicken stock
2 bay leaves
2 sprigs fresh thyme
2 large zucchini (300g), chopped coarsely
200g green beans, trimmed, cut into 3cm lengths
2 medium tomatoes (300g), chopped coarsely
300ml cream
1 tablespoon wholegrain mustard

1 Coat chicken in flour; shake off excess. Heat half the oil in large saucepan; cook chicken, in batches, until browned.
2 Heat remaining oil in same pan; cook onion, garlic, carrot, potato and celery, stirring, about 5 minutes or until vegetables are browned lightly. Add wine; bring to the boil. Boil, uncovered, until liquid reduces by half.
3 Return chicken to pan with stock, bay leaves and thyme; bring to the boil. Reduce heat; simmer, covered, about 30 minutes or until chicken is tender. Add zucchini, beans, tomato, cream and mustard; simmer, uncovered, about 15 minutes or until vegetables are tender and sauce thickens slightly.
4 Serve bowls of creamy chicken casserole with steamed white rice or small pasta shells.
preparation time 30 minutes
cooking time 1 hour **serves** 4
nutritional count per serving 60.7g total fat (28.4g saturated fat); 3900kJ (933 cal); 28.1g carbohydrate; 56.1g protein; 8.5g fibre
note Recipe is not suitable to freeze.

seafood chowder

300g small mussels
500g uncooked medium prawns
40g butter
1 small leek (200g), sliced thinly
2 cloves garlic, crushed
2 rindless bacon rashers (130g), chopped finely
2 tablespoons plain flour
3 cups (750ml) milk
1 cup (250ml) vegetable stock
200g baby squid hoods, sliced thinly
300g firm white fish fillets, chopped coarsely
2 tablespoons finely chopped fresh chives

1 Scrub mussels; remove beards. Shell and devein prawns, leaving tails intact.
2 Melt butter in large saucepan; cook leek, garlic and bacon, stirring, until leek softens.
3 Add flour to pan; cook, stirring 1 minute. Stir in milk and stock; bring to the boil. Reduce heat; simmer, uncovered, 10 minutes.
4 Add seafood; simmer, uncovered, about 4 minutes or until prawns change colour and mussels open (discard any that do not). Serve chowder sprinkled with chives.
preparation time 30 minutes
cooking time 20 minutes **serves** 4
nutritional count per serving 23.7g total fat (13.1g saturated fat); 2061kJ (493 cal); 15.8g carbohydrate; 53.3g protein; 1.4g fibre
note Recipe is not suitable to freeze.

tip Fish stock can be used instead of vegetable stock.

hearty winter soup

2 tablespoons olive oil
1kg gravy beef, trimmed, cut into 2cm pieces
12 shallots (300g), halved
2 cloves garlic, crushed
2 small parsnips (240g), chopped coarsely
2 small turnips (300g), chopped coarsely
2 medium swedes (450g), chopped coarsely
300g piece pumpkin, chopped coarsely
1 cup (250ml) dry white wine
3 cups (750ml) beef stock
3 cups (750ml) water
1 tablespoon tomato paste
4 sprigs fresh thyme
⅓ cup short-cut vermicelli

1 Heat half the oil in large saucepan; cook beef, in batches, until browned.
2 Heat remaining oil in same pan; cook shallots and garlic, stirring, until onion softens.
3 Add vegetables, wine, stock, the water, paste and thyme; bring to the boil. Reduce heat; simmer, covered, 1½ hours, stirring occasionally.
4 Add vermicelli; cook, uncovered, about 10 minutes or until just softened.

preparation time 25 minutes
cooking time 2 hours **serves** 4
nutritional count per serving 21.4g total fat (6.5g saturated fat); 2387kJ (571 cal); 22g carbohydrate; 58.5g protein; 7.6g fibre
note Recipe is not suitable to freeze.

prosciutto-wrapped pork and veal meatloaf

4 slices white bread (180g)
½ cup (125ml) milk
300g pork mince
450g veal mince
1 small leek (200g), chopped finely
2 cloves garlic, crushed
2 teaspoons fresh thyme leaves
½ cup finely chopped fresh flat-leaf parsley
½ cup (40g) finely grated parmesan cheese
2 eggs
8 slices prosciutto (120g)
1 tablespoon dijon mustard

1 Preheat oven to 200°C/180°C fan-forced.
2 Remove crusts from bread; tear bread into pieces. Pour milk over bread in large bowl; stand 2 minutes.
3 Add minces, leek, garlic, herbs, cheese and eggs to bowl; mix well. Roughly shape mixture into a mound.
4 Lay 6 slices of prosciutto on board, overlapping slightly; brush with mustard. Place mince mound onto prosciutto slices; using wet hands, pat mixture into loaf shape. Lay remaining 2 slices prosciutto lengthways on top of meatloaf. Wrap bottom prosciutto slices around sides of meatloaf to meet slices on top. Turn meatloaf over carefully; place on wire rack set in large shallow baking dish.
5 Cook meatloaf, uncovered, about 1 hour or until juices run clear. Cover meatloaf; stand 10 minutes before serving.

preparation time 20 minutes
cooking time 1 hour **serves** 4
nutritional count per serving 23.4g total fat (9.6g saturated fat); 2266kJ (542 cal); 23.4g carbohydrate; 58g protein; 2.9g fibre
note Recipe is not suitable to freeze.

tomato-braised lamb shanks

1 tablespoon olive oil
4 french-trimmed lamb shanks (1kg)
1 medium brown onion (150g), sliced thinly
2 medium carrots (240g), chopped finely
2 trimmed celery stalks (200g), sliced thinly
2 cloves garlic, crushed
½ cup (125ml) dry red wine
1¾ cup (430ml) beef stock
4 medium tomatoes (600g), chopped coarsely
410g can crushed tomatoes
2 tablespoons tomato paste
4 sprigs fresh thyme

1 Heat oil in large saucepan; cook lamb, in batches, until browned.
2 Cook onion, carrot, celery and garlic in same pan, stirring, until celery softens.
3 Return lamb to pan with wine, stock, fresh and undrained tomatoes, paste and thyme; bring to the boil. Reduce heat; simmer, covered, 1 hour, stirring occasionally. Uncover; simmer about 1 hour or until lamb is tender.

preparation time 20 minutes
cooking time 2 hours **serves** 4
nutritional count per serving 7.7g total fat (1.9g saturated fat); 1250kJ (299 cal); 13.2g carbohydrate; 35.2g protein; 6.8g fibre
note Recipe is suitable to freeze.

minted broad bean and ham soup

2 teaspoons olive oil
1 large brown onion (200g), chopped coarsely
2 trimmed celery stalks (200g), chopped coarsely
1 medium carrot (120g), chopped coarsely
2 cloves garlic, crushed
1kg ham hock
2 litres (8 cups) water
3 cups (450g) frozen broad beans, peeled
1 tablespoon lemon juice
⅓ cup finely chopped fresh mint

1 Heat oil in large saucepan; cook onion, celery, carrot and garlic, stirring, until vegetables soften. Add ham hock and the water; bring to the boil. Reduce heat; simmer, covered, 1½ hours. Uncover; simmer 30 minutes.
2 Remove ham hock from soup; when cool enough to handle, remove meat from bone, shred coarsely. Discard skin and bone.
3 Meanwhile, add beans to soup; simmer, uncovered, 5 minutes or until beans are tender. Cool 5 minutes.
4 Using hand-held blender, puree soup, in pan, until soup is almost smooth. Return ham meat to soup with juice; cook, stirring, until hot. Serve soup sprinkled with mint.

preparation time 30 minutes
cooking time 2 hours 30 minutes **serves** 4
nutritional count per serving 7.4g total fat (2g saturated fat); 890kJ (213 cal); 13.4g carbohydrate; 17.7g protein; 11.4g fibre
note Recipe is suitable to freeze.

mushroom, spinach and chickpea soup

1 tablespoon olive oil
1 medium brown onion (150g), chopped finely
2 cloves garlic, crushed
200g button mushrooms, sliced thinly
200g swiss brown mushrooms, sliced thinly
1 litre (4 cups) chicken stock
400g can chickpeas, rinsed, drained
410g can crushed tomatoes
100g baby spinach leaves

1 Heat oil in large saucepan; cook onion and garlic, stirring, until onion softens.
2 Add mushrooms; cook, stirring, until tender. Add stock, chickpeas and undrained tomatoes; bring to the boil. Reduce heat; simmer, covered, 20 minutes.
3 Stir in spinach; serve soup as soon as spinach wilts.
preparation time 15 minutes
cooking time 40 minutes **serves** 4
nutritional count per serving 7.6g total fat
(1.4g saturated fat); 836kJ (200 cal);
16.6g carbohydrate; 12.6g protein; 8.2g fibre
note Recipe is not suitable to freeze.

country-style beef and potato casserole

1kg beef chuck steak, cut into 2cm pieces
½ cup (75g) plain flour, approximately
2 tablespoons olive oil
3 small brown onion (450g), halved
2 cloves garlic, crushed
2 rindless bacon rashers (130g), chopped coarsely
2 tablespoons tomato paste
3 cups (750ml) beef stock
410g can crushed tomatoes
¼ cup (60ml) worcestershire sauce
2 medium potatoes (400g), chopped coarsely
1 medium kumara (400g), chopped coarsely
1 large red capsicum (350g), chopped coarsely
1 tablespoon coarsely chopped fresh thyme

1 Coat beef in flour, shake away excess. Heat oil in large saucepan; cook beef, in batches, until browned.
2 Cook onion, garlic and bacon in same pan, stirring, until bacon crisps. Add paste; cook, stirring, 1 minute.
3 Return beef to pan with stock, undrained tomatoes and sauce; bring to the boil. Reduce heat; simmer, covered, 1 hour, stirring occasionally.
4 Add potato, kumara and capsicum to pan; simmer, uncovered, stirring occasionally, about 30 minutes or until beef is tender. Serve casserole sprinkled with thyme.
preparation time 35 minutes
cooking time 2 hours **serves** 6
nutritional count per serving 17.3g total fat
(5.2g saturated fat); 2036kJ (487 cal);
34.5g carbohydrate; 45.5g protein; 4.8g fibre
note Recipe is not suitable to freeze.

leg of lamb on lemon-scented potatoes

4 slices pancetta (60g), chopped finely
2 cloves garlic, crushed
1 tablespoon finely chopped fresh rosemary
1 tablespoon finely grated lemon rind
1.2kg easy-carve leg of lamb
6 medium potatoes (1.2kg), sliced thinly
¼ cup (60ml) lemon juice
1 cup (250ml) chicken stock
25g butter, chopped coarsely
1 lemon, cut into wedges

1 Preheat oven to 220°C/200°C fan-forced.
2 Combine pancetta, garlic, rosemary and rind
in small bowl.
3 Using sharp knife, pierce lamb all over; press
pancetta mixture into cuts.
4 Place potato in large baking dish; drizzle with juice
and stock, dot with butter.
5 Place lamb on potato; roast 20 minutes. Reduce
temperature to 180°C/160°C fan-forced; roast about
1 hour or until lamb is cooked as desired. Cover lamb,
stand 10 minutes before slicing. Serve lamb with potatoes
and lemon wedges.

preparation time 20 minutes

cooking time 1 hour 20 minutes **serves** 6

nutritional count per serving 12.4g total fat
(6.1g saturated fat); 1547kJ (370 cal);
23.3g carbohydrate; 39.3g protein; 3.3g fibre

note Recipe is not suitable to freeze.

scotch broth

1kg lamb neck chops
2 litres (8 cups) water
½ cup (100g) pearl barley
1 medium brown onion (150g), chopped finely
1 medium carrot (120g), chopped finely
1 medium turnip (230g), chopped finely
1 trimmed celery stalk (100g), chopped finely
2 cups (160g) finely shredded cabbage
½ cup (60g) frozen peas
¼ cup coarsely chopped fresh flat-leaf parsley

1 Combine lamb, the water and barley in large saucepan;
bring to the boil. Reduce heat; simmer, covered, 1 hour,
skimming fat from surface occasionally.
2 Add onion, carrot, turnip and celery; simmer, covered,
about 30 minutes or until vegetables are tender.
3 Remove lamb from pan. When cool enough to handle,
remove and discard bones; shred meat coarsely.
4 Return meat to soup with cabbage and peas; simmer,
uncovered, about 10 minutes or until cabbage is just
tender. Stir in parsley.

preparation time 30 minutes

cooking time 1 hour 45 minutes **serves** 4

nutritional count per serving 23.9g total fat
(10.6g saturated fat); 2036kJ (487 cal);
22.6g carbohydrate; 41.4g protein; 8.5g fibre

note Recipe is not suitable to freeze.

tip Make recipe a day ahead; keep, covered, in the refrigerator.
Skim fat from surface of broth before reheating and serving.

The culinary masterminds of France have produced countless classic recipes. For one-pot cooking, French provincial dishes can't be beaten with their simple methods and big flavours.

FRENCH

duck and caramelised apple salad

4 duck breasts (600g)
2 medium apples (300g), cut into thin wedges
2 tablespoons caster sugar
150g curly endive, trimmed
½ cup (70g) coarsely chopped roasted hazelnuts
½ cup loosely packed fresh mint leaves
1 tablespoon sherry vinegar
1 tablespoon olive oil

1 Using a sharp knife, score skin on each duck breast in a 1.5cm diamond pattern.
2 Heat large frying pan to very hot. Place duck breasts, skin-side down, in pan; cook about 10 minutes or until skin is golden and crisp. Turn breasts over; cook 2 minutes then remove from pan. Stand duck breasts, covered, 10 minutes.
3 Meanwhile, cook apple in same cleaned pan, stirring, 2 minutes. Add sugar; cook, stirring, about 3 minutes or until apple is browned and tender.
4 Arrange endive, nuts and mint on serving plates. Slice duck breasts thinly then arrange on salad with apple; drizzle with combined vinegar and oil.

preparation time 15 minutes
cooking time 15 minutes **serves** 4
nutritional count per serving 70.9g total fat (17.8g saturated fat); 3348kJ (801 cal); 17.6g carbohydrate; 23.2g protein; 4.3g fibre
note Recipe is not suitable to freeze.

tip Sherry vinegar is a natural vinegar made from the sherry grape grown in the southwest of Spain; aged in oak, this traditional wine vinegar has a mellow sweet-sour taste, similar to balsamic, which makes it a perfect dressing for tender young greens, like the endive and mint used here.

tip Food referred to as "à la bourguignon" is food cooked in the style of the famous French wine region of Burgundy, and is instantly recognisable by its red wine sauce containing mushrooms, bacon and onions. While most of us are familiar with the classic boeuf (beef) bourguignon, lamb shanks given a similar culinary treatment are deserving of the same praise.

chicken with fennel and orange

1 tablespoon olive oil

20g butter

12 chicken drumsticks (1.8kg)

4 baby fennel bulbs (520g), trimmed, quartered

1 medium brown onion (150g), chopped finely

2 cloves garlic, crushed

1 tablespoon finely grated orange rind

1 cup (250ml) orange juice

1 cup (250ml) dry white wine

2 cups (500ml) chicken stock

6 fresh sprigs thyme

1 medium kumara (400g), chopped coarsely

1 Heat oil and butter in large deep saucepan; cook chicken, in batches, until well browned. Discard all but 1 tablespoon of the pan drippings. Reheat dripping in same pan; cook fennel, in batches, until browned and caramelised.

2 Cook onion and garlic in same pan, stirring, until onion softens. Return chicken and fennel to pan with rind, juice, wine, stock and thyme; bring to the boil. Reduce heat; simmer, covered, about 30 minutes or until chicken is cooked.

3 Add kumara; simmer, uncovered, about 20 minutes or until kumara is tender. Discard thyme before serving. Serve with pasta such as tagliatelle or fettuccine.

preparation time 20 minutes

cooking time 1 hour **serves** 4

nutritional count per serving 40.9g total fat (13.1g saturated fat); 3031kJ (725 cal); 22.8g carbohydrate; 55g protein; 4.6g fibre

note Recipe is not suitable to freeze.

lamb shanks bourguignon

12 baby onions (300g)

8 french-trimmed lamb shanks (2kg)

¼ cup (35g) plain flour

1 tablespoon olive oil

20g butter

6 rindless bacon rashers (390g), chopped coarsely

300g mushrooms

2 cloves garlic, crushed

1 cup (250ml) dry red wine

1 cup (250ml) beef stock

1 cup (250ml) water

2 tablespoons tomato paste

2 bay leaves

1 tablespoon brown sugar

1 Preheat oven to 180°C/160°C fan-forced.

2 Peel onions, leaving root ends intact.

3 Coat lamb in flour; shake off excess. Heat oil in large flameproof casserole dish; cook lamb, in batches, until browned.

4 Melt butter in same dish; cook onions, bacon, mushrooms and garlic, stirring, until vegetables are browned lightly.

5 Return lamb to dish with wine, stock, the water, paste, bay leaves and sugar; bring to the boil. Cover dish; transfer to oven. Cook 1½ hours. Uncover; cook about 30 minutes or until lamb is tender and sauce thickens slightly.

6 Divide lamb among serving bowls; drizzle with sauce. Serve with mashed potato.

preparation time 30 minutes

cooking time 2 hours **serves** 4

nutritional count per serving 37.5g total fat (15.2g saturated fat); 3248kJ (777 cal); 15.5g carbohydrate; 82.3g protein; 3.8g fibre

note Recipe is not suitable to freeze.

fish stew with saffron, tomato and wine

500g uncooked medium king prawns
500g small mussels
1 tablespoon olive oil
1 medium brown onion (150g), chopped finely
3 cloves garlic, crushed
1 small leek (200g), sliced thinly
1 small fennel bulb (200g), sliced thinly
1 trimmed celery stalk (100g), sliced thinly
½ cup (125ml) dry white wine
2 x 400g cans diced tomatoes
1 litre (4 cups) fish stock
pinch saffron threads
200g kipfler potatoes, cut into 1cm slices
300g skinless firm white fish fillet, chopped coarsely
300g skinless salmon fillet, chopped coarsely

1 Shell and devein prawns. Scrub mussels; remove beards.
2 Heat oil in large flameproof casserole dish; cook onion, garlic, leek, fennel and celery, stirring, about 10 minutes or until vegetables soften.
3 Add wine, undrained tomatoes, stock, saffron and potato to pan; bring to the boil. Reduce heat; simmer, uncovered, about 10 minutes or until potato is tender.
4 Add prawns and fish fillets to pan; cook, uncovered, 5 minutes. Add mussels; cook, covered, about 2 minutes or until mussels open (discard any that do not).

preparation time 30 minutes
cooking time 30 minutes **serves** 6
nutritional count per serving 9g total fat
(1.9g saturated fat); 1254kJ (300 cal);
13.5g carbohydrate; 35.4g protein; 4.3g fibre
note Recipe is not suitable to freeze.

ratatouille with gremolata and goats cheese

1 tablespoon olive oil
1 medium brown onion (150g), chopped coarsely
1 clove garlic, crushed
2 large zucchini (300g), sliced thickly
1 medium eggplant (300g), chopped coarsely
1 medium red capsicum (200g), sliced thinly
1 medium green capsicum (200g), sliced thinly
150g mushrooms, halved
4 medium tomatoes (600g), chopped coarsely
410g can crushed tomatoes
½ cup (125ml) water
¼ cup finely chopped fresh flat-leaf parsley
2 teaspoons finely grated lemon rind
125g piece goats cheese, crumbled

1 Heat oil in large saucepan; cook onion and garlic, stirring, until onion softens.
2 Add zucchini, eggplant, capsicums, mushrooms, fresh and undrained crushed tomatoes and the water to pan; bring to the boil. Reduce heat; simmer, uncovered, about 30 minutes or until vegetables are tender and sauce thickens slightly.
3 To make gremolata, combine parsley and rind in small bowl.
4 Divide ratatouille among serving bowls; sprinkle with gremolata then cheese.

preparation time 20 minutes
cooking time 35 minutes **serves** 4
nutritional count per serving 10.6g total fat
(3.9g saturated fat); 899kJ (215 cal);
14.4g carbohydrate; 11.4g protein; 8.6g fibre

tip As a general rule, we do not recommend freezing cooked seafood of any kind because it tends to undergo both textural and flavour changes.

tip Gremolata's popularity has seen it morph into myriad guises well removed from its original use as a simple garnish strewn over steaming osso buco or, as we have done here, with the ratatouille. Today, gremolata is made from any number of aromatic ingredients and served with many different dishes. Olive, rocket, coriander, rosemary, breadcrumb, shallots, orange and lime, even chilli, gremolatas are not unusual, seen sprinkled over everything from soups to steamed vegetables.

tip Lamb noisettes are lamb sirloin chops with the bone removed and the "tail" wrapped around the meaty part of the chop and secured with a toothpick.

chicken and artichoke fricassée

2 tablespoons olive oil

8 chicken drumsticks (1.2kg)

1 medium brown onion (150g), chopped finely

4 cloves garlic, crushed

½ cup (125ml) dry white wine

1½ cups (375ml) chicken stock

1 tablespoon finely grated lemon rind

1 tablespoon lemon juice

300ml cream

125g baby spinach leaves

2 x 340g jars marinated artichokes in oil, drained, halved

1 tablespoon finely chopped fresh oregano

1 tablespoon fresh oregano leaves

1 Heat half the oil in large saucepan; cook chicken, in batches, until browned.

2 Heat remaining oil in same pan; cook onion and garlic, stirring, until onion softens. Add wine, stock, rind and juice; bring to the boil. Return chicken to pan; reduce heat, simmer, covered, 20 minutes. Uncover; simmer, about 10 minutes or until chicken is cooked through.

3 Remove chicken from pan, place two drumsticks in each serving bowl.

4 Combine cream, spinach, artichokes and chopped oregano in pan with sauce mixture; bring to the boil. Reduce heat; simmer, uncovered, about 2 minutes or until sauce thickens slightly. Pour sauce over chicken; sprinkle with oregano leaves. Serve with steamed white rice.

preparation time 10 minutes

cooking time 1 hour **serves** 4

nutritional count per serving 65.4g total fat (29.8g saturated fat); 3315kJ (793 cal); 7.4g carbohydrate; 39.4g protein; 2g fibre

note Recipe is not suitable to freeze.

navarin of lamb

2 tablespoons olive oil

8 lamb noisettes (800g)

1 large brown onion (200g), sliced thickly

2 cloves garlic, crushed

2 tablespoons plain flour

1 cup (250ml) water

3 cups (750ml) chicken stock

½ cup (125ml) dry red wine

400g can diced tomatoes

¼ cup (70g) tomato paste

2 bay leaves

2 sprigs fresh rosemary

2 trimmed celery stalks (200g), cut into 5cm lengths

150g green beans, trimmed, halved

20 baby carrots (400g), trimmed

200g mushrooms

1 cup (120g) frozen peas

½ cup coarsely chopped fresh flat-leaf parsley

1 Heat oil in large saucepan; cook lamb, in batches, until browned. Cook onion and garlic in same pan, stirring, until onion softens. Add flour; cook, stirring, until mixture bubbles and thickens. Gradually add the water, stock and wine; stir until mixture boils and thickens.

2 Return lamb to pan with undrained tomatoes, paste, bay leaves and rosemary; bring to the boil. Reduce heat; simmer, covered, 30 minutes.

3 Add celery, beans, carrots and mushrooms to pan; simmer, covered, about 30 minutes or until vegetables are tender. Add peas; simmer, uncovered, until peas are just tender.

4 Remove and discard toothpicks from lamb. Serve bowls of navarin sprinkled with parsley and, if you like, creamy celeriac mash.

preparation time 20 minutes

cooking time 1 hour 30 minutes **serves** 4

nutritional count per serving 32.6g total fat (12.9g saturated fat); 2913kJ (697 cal); 21.4g carbohydrate; 69.3g protein; 11g fibre

note Recipe is suitable to freeze at the end of step 3.

veal schnitzels with potatoes and bacon

60g butter
3 medium potatoes (600g), cut into 1cm cubes
3 rindless bacon rashers (200g), chopped coarsely
⅔ cup (160ml) chicken stock
8 thin veal schnitzels (640g)
¼ cup (35g) plain flour
½ cup (125ml) dry white wine
½ cup (125ml) cream
2 teaspoons wholegrain mustard

1 Heat half the butter in large frying pan; cook potato and bacon, stirring, about 10 minutes or until bacon crisps. Add stock; cook, covered, about 10 minutes or until potato is tender and liquid is absorbed. Remove from pan; cover to keep warm.

2 Coat veal in flour; shake off excess. Heat remaining butter in same pan; cook veal, in batches, until cooked as desired. Cover to keep warm.

3 Add wine to same pan; cook, stirring, until reduced by half. Add cream and mustard; simmer, uncovered, about 3 minutes or until sauce thickens slightly.

4 Serve veal with sauce and potatoes.

preparation time 20 minutes
cooking time 35 minutes **serves** 4
nutritional count per serving 36.7g total fat (20.7g saturated fat); 2717kJ (650 cal); 24.5g carbohydrate; 49.3g protein; 2.4g fibre
note Recipe is not suitable to freeze.

provençale beef casserole

2 tablespoons olive oil

1kg gravy beef, cut into 2cm pieces

2 rindless bacon rashers (130g), chopped finely

1 medium leek (350g), sliced thinly

2 medium carrots (240g), chopped coarsely

1 trimmed celery stalk (100g), chopped coarsely

2 cloves garlic, crushed

410g can crushed tomatoes

1½ cups (375ml) beef stock

1 cup (250ml) dry red wine

2 bay leaves

4 sprigs fresh thyme

6 sprigs fresh flat-leaf parsley

2 medium zucchini (240g), sliced thickly

½ cup (75g) seeded black olives

1 Heat oil in large saucepan; cook beef, in batches, until browned.

2 Cook bacon, leek, carrot, celery and garlic in same pan, stirring, until leek softens.

3 Return beef to pan with undrained tomatoes, stock, wine, bay leaves, thyme and parsley; bring to the boil. Reduce heat; simmer, covered, 1 hour, stirring occasionally.

4 Add zucchini and olives; simmer, covered, about 30 minutes or until beef is tender.

5 Remove and discard bay leaves, thyme and parsley before serving with crushed kipfler potatoes.

preparation time 30 minutes

cooking time 2 hours **serves** 4

nutritional count per serving 25.8g total fat (7.8g saturated fat); 2458kJ (588 cal); 14.1g carbohydrate; 61.4g protein; 6.4g fibre

note Recipe is suitable to freeze at the end of step 3.

steamed mussels in tomato garlic broth

1 tablespoon olive oil

2 shallots (50g), chopped finely

4 cloves garlic, crushed

410g can crushed tomatoes

1 cup (250ml) dry white wine

1 teaspoon caster sugar

2kg small black mussels

½ cup coarsely chopped fresh flat-leaf parsley

1 Heat oil in large saucepan; cook shallot and garlic, stirring, until shallot softens.

2 Add undrained tomatoes, wine and sugar; bring to the boil. Reduce heat; simmer, uncovered, about 10 minutes or until sauce thickens slightly.

3 Meanwhile, scrub mussels; remove beards. Add mussels to pan; simmer, covered, about 5 minutes, shaking pan occasionally, until mussels open (discard any that do not). Remove mussels from pan, divide among serving bowls; cover with foil to keep warm.

4 Bring tomato mixture to the boil; boil, uncovered, about 5 minutes or until sauce thickens slightly. Pour tomato mixture over mussels; sprinkle with parsley.

preparation time 25 minutes

cooking time 30 minutes **serves** 4

nutritional count per serving 6.7g total fat (1.2g saturated fat); 828kJ (198 cal); 9.9g carbohydrate; 13.3g protein; 2.2g fibre

note Recipe is not suitable to freeze.

tip The French love a good leg of lamb, and one of their classic ways of cooking is "á la bretonne", as it is prepared in Brittany, the northern French province known for its love affair with all bean varieties. You can use canned cannellini, navy, great northern or butter beans in this recipe.

lamb bretonne

1.5kg leg of lamb
1 clove garlic, sliced thinly
2 sprigs fresh rosemary
1 teaspoon sea salt flakes
½ teaspoon freshly cracked black pepper
20g butter
2 medium brown onions (300g), sliced thinly
3 cloves garlic, crushed
410g can crushed tomatoes
410g can tomato puree
2 cups (500ml) beef stock
400g can white beans, rinsed, drained

1 Preheat oven to 180°C/160°C fan-forced.
2 Trim excess fat from lamb. Pierce lamb in several places with sharp knife; press sliced garlic and a little of the rosemary firmly into cuts. Rub salt and pepper over lamb.
3 Heat butter in large flameproof baking dish; cook onion and crushed garlic, stirring, until onion browns slightly. Stir in undrained tomatoes, puree, stock, beans and remaining rosemary; bring to the boil then remove from heat.
4 Place lamb, pierced-side down, on bean mixture, cover; transfer to oven. Cook 1 hour. Uncover, turn lamb carefully; cook, brushing occasionally with tomato mixture, about 1 hour or until lamb is cooked as desired.
preparation time 20 minutes
cooking time 2 hours 10 minutes **serves** 4
nutritional count per serving 19.9g total fat (9.5g saturated fat); 2324kJ (556 cal); 20.2g carbohydrate; 69.8g protein; 7.7g fibre
note Recipe is not suitable to freeze.

rabbit stew

2 tablespoons oil
1kg rabbit pieces
3 medium brown onions (450g), sliced thickly
4 cloves garlic, crushed
1 cup (250ml) water
1 litre (4 cups) chicken stock
410g can diced tomatoes
5 medium potatoes (1kg), chopped coarsely
2 medium carrots (240g), sliced thickly
1 tablespoon balsamic vinegar
3 bay leaves
1 teaspoon dried chilli flakes
⅓ cup coarsely chopped fresh mint
1 cup (120g) frozen peas

1 Heat half the oil in large saucepan; cook rabbit, in batches, until browned.
2 Heat remaining oil in same pan; cook onion and garlic, stirring, until onion softens.
3 Add the water, stock, undrained tomatoes, potato, carrot, vinegar, bay leaves, chilli and mint to pan. Return rabbit to pan; bring to the boil. Reduce heat; simmer, uncovered, 1¼ hours. Add peas; simmer, uncovered, 5 minutes.

preparation time 20 minutes
cooking time 1 hour 45 minutes **serves** 4
nutritional count per serving 19.4g total fat
(5.1g saturated fat); 2750kJ (658 cal);
44.4g carbohydrate; 70.7g protein; 10.6g fibre
note Recipe is not suitable to freeze.

pork neck, orange and white bean stew

1 tablespoon olive oil
800g pork neck, cut into 3cm pieces
1 large celeriac (750g), trimmed, peeled, chopped coarsely
3 medium carrots (360g), chopped coarsely
3 cloves garlic, peeled
1 cup (250ml) dry white wine
1 cup (250ml) chicken stock
3 x 5cm strips orange rind
½ cup (125ml) orange juice
400g can cannellini beans, rinsed, drained

1 Heat oil in large flameproof casserole dish; cook pork, in batches, until browned. Add vegetables, garlic, wine, stock, rind and juice to dish; bring to the boil. Return pork to dish, reduce heat; simmer, covered, 40 minutes.
2 Add beans to dish; simmer, uncovered, about 20 minutes or until pork is tender.

preparation time 25 minutes
cooking time 1 hour 15 minutes **serves** 4
nutritional count per serving 21.4g total fat
(6.2g saturated fat); 2215kJ (530 cal);
18.1g carbohydrate; 50g protein; 12.7g fibre
note Recipe is not suitable to freeze.

Rich tomato sauce, smoky meat, herbs and cheese – the very best of fresh ingredients – that's the Italian way. Put the pot on and let it bubble its way to a delicious infusion of flavours.

ITALIAN

spaghetti marinara with crab

4 uncooked blue swimmer crabs (1.3kg)
1 tablespoon olive oil
1 medium brown onion (150g), chopped finely
1 clove garlic, crushed
1 fresh long red chilli, chopped finely
400g can diced tomatoes
½ cup finely chopped fresh flat-leaf parsley
1 litre (4 cups) water
500g spaghetti
½ cup firmly packed fresh flat-leaf parsley leaves

1 Place crabs in large container filled with ice and water; stand 1 hour. Slide knife under tail flap of crabs; in a peeling motion, lift off and discard back shell. Discard gills, liver and brain matter; rinse crabs under cold water. Using cleaver or heavy knife, chop each body into quarters.

2 Heat oil in large saucepan; cook onion, garlic and chilli, stirring, until onion softens. Add undrained tomatoes, crab and chopped parsley; cook, covered, stirring occasionally, until crab changes colour.

3 Add the water to pan; bring to the boil. Add pasta; once pasta begins to soften, mix gently into crab mixture. Boil, uncovered, stirring regularly, about 10 minutes or until pasta is tender and sauce thickens.

4 Serve bowls of pasta sprinkled with parsley.

preparation time 20 minutes
cooking time 30 minutes **serves** 4
nutritional count per serving 6.9g total fat
(1g saturated fat); 2370kJ (567 cal);
91.9g carbohydrate; 27.7g protein; 11g fibre
note Recipe is not suitable to freeze.

tips Stand uncooked pasta upright in the mixture until the bottom half is soft enough to bend without breaking, then stir it into the crab mixture, stirring regularly so it cooks evenly. You will need to use your fingers to eat the crab, so serve the marinara with finger bowls and large napkins, as well as forks and spoons.

tip Bollito misto, which translates as "boiled mixed meats", is a traditional North Italian dish served on New Year's Eve and other special occasions. It is made by boiling large cuts of beef, veal, poultry, pork and various Italian sausages in flavoured stock. The meat is then carved and served with some of the stock and one of a selection of traditional condiments, most often salsa verde or mostarda di frutta (pickled fruits). Our one-pot version of this classic dish cooks the meats already cut and the piquant flavours of anchovies and capers are stirred straight into the pan.

bollito misto

2 tablespoons olive oil
4 thin italian pork sausages (320g)
500g beef chuck steak, cut into 2cm pieces
500g chicken thigh fillets, cut into 2cm pieces
1 medium brown onion (150g), chopped coarsely
1 clove garlic, crushed
2 cups (500ml) beef stock
1 cup (250ml) water
2 bay leaves
2 medium carrots (240g), chopped coarsely
2 medium potatoes (400g), chopped coarsely
¼ cup (50g) capers, rinsed, drained, chopped coarsely
4 anchovy fillets, chopped finely
2 teaspoons finely grated lemon rind
1 tablespoon lemon juice
1 cup coarsely chopped fresh flat-leaf parsley

1 Heat half the oil in large saucepan; cook sausages until browned. Remove from pan; chop coarsely.
2 Cook beef and chicken, in batches, in same pan, until browned.
3 Heat remaining oil in same pan; cook onion and garlic, stirring, until onion softens. Return meats to pan with stock, the water and bay leaves; bring to the boil. Reduce heat; simmer, covered, 1½ hours.
4 Add carrot and potato to pan; simmer, uncovered, about 30 minutes or until vegetables soften. Add capers, anchovy, rind and juice; cook, stirring, until hot. Remove from heat; stir in parsley.

preparation time 30 minutes
cooking time 2 hours 30 minutes **serves** 4
nutritional count per serving 42.2g total fat (13.8g saturated fat); 3035kJ (726 cal); 20.5g carbohydrate; 64.1g protein; 5.7g fibre
note Recipe is not suitable to freeze.

baked prawn, asparagus and broad bean risotto

You will need about 500g fresh broad beans in the pod to get the required amount of shelled beans.

1 tablespoon olive oil
1 large brown onion (200g), chopped finely
2 cloves garlic, crushed
2 cups (400g) arborio rice
½ cup (125ml) dry white wine
1 litre (4 cups) chicken stock
1½ cups (375ml) water
1 tablespoon finely grated lemon rind
⅓ cup (80ml) lemon juice
1kg uncooked medium king prawns
170g asparagus, trimmed, cut into 3cm lengths
1 cup (150g) shelled, peeled fresh broad beans
⅓ cup coarsely chopped fresh mint

1 Preheat oven to 180°C/160°C fan-forced.
2 Heat oil in shallow large flameproof baking dish; cook onion and garlic, stirring, until onion softens. Add rice; stir to coat in onion mixture. Add wine; bring to the boil. Boil, uncovered, stirring, until liquid is absorbed. Stir in stock, the water, rind and juice; bring to the boil. Cover tightly, transfer to oven; cook 25 minutes, stirring halfway through cooking time.
3 Meanwhile, shell and devein prawns, leaving tails intact.
4 Uncover risotto, return to oven; cook 15 minutes. Stir in prawns, asparagus and broad beans, return to oven; cook, uncovered, about 10 minutes or until prawns change colour and rice is tender.
5 Serve bowls of risotto sprinkled with mint.

preparation time 15 minutes

cooking time 1 hour **serves** 4

nutritional count per serving 7.2g total fat (1.4g saturated fat); 2512kJ (601 cal); 85.9g carbohydrate; 39.5g protein; 4.9g fibre

note Recipe is not suitable to freeze.

beef and mushrooms in red wine

2 tablespoons olive oil
1kg beef blade steak, diced into 2cm pieces
4 medium brown onions (600g), chopped coarsely
200g mushrooms, halved
2⅓ cups (580ml) dry red wine
¼ cup (60ml) beef stock
2 x 410g cans crushed tomatoes
1 tablespoon brown sugar
3 sprigs fresh rosemary
2 tablespoons fresh oregano leaves

1 Heat half the oil in large flameproof casserole dish; cook beef, in batches, until browned.
2 Heat remaining oil in same pan; cook onion, stirring, 2 minutes. Add mushrooms; cook, stirring, 2 minutes.
3 Return beef to pan with wine, stock, undrained tomatoes, sugar, rosemary and half the oregano; bring to the boil. Reduce heat; simmer, covered, 1 hour, stirring occasionally. Uncover; simmer 15 minutes. Serve beef sprinkled with remaining oregano, and accompanied with a loaf of ciabatta bread.

preparation time 15 minutes

cooking time 1 hour 30 minutes **serves** 4

nutritional count per serving 26g total fat (8.3g saturated fat); 2332kJ (558 cal); 17.7g carbohydrate; 58.1g protein; 5.7g fibre

note Recipe is not suitable to freeze.

veal rolls with prosciutto and sage

4 slices prosciutto (60g), halved crossways
8 veal schnitzels (800g)
8 slices swiss cheese (170g)
8 large fresh sage leaves
2 tablespoons olive oil
1 medium onion (150g), chopped finely
2 cloves garlic, crushed
4 anchovy fillets, chopped finely
¼ cup (60ml) dry white wine
1½ cups (375ml) beef stock
2 x 410g cans crushed tomatoes
800g kipfler potatoes, halved lengthways
1 tablespoon rinsed, drained baby capers
⅓ cup (40g) seeded black olives
½ cup firmly packed fresh basil leaves

1 Preheat oven to 200°C/180°C fan-forced.
2 Place one slice prosciutto on each schnitzel; top each with one slice of cheese and one sage leaf. Roll schnitzels to enclose filling; secure with toothpicks.
3 Heat half the oil in large flameproof casserole dish; cook veal, in batches, until browned all over.
4 Heat remaining oil in same dish; cook onion, garlic and anchovy, stirring, until onion softens.
5 Add wine, stock, undrained tomatoes, potato, capers, olives and half the basil. Return veal to dish; bring to the boil. Cover dish; transfer to oven. Cook about 30 minutes or until potato is tender. Serve veal rolls sprinkled with remaining basil.

preparation time 20 minutes
cooking time 40 minutes **serves** 4
nutritional count per serving 28.7g total fat
(11.3g saturated fat); 2947kJ (705 cal);
38.1g carbohydrate; 67.2g protein; 7.5g fibre
note Recipe is not suitable to freeze.

quail cacciatore

8 quails (1.3kg)
8 slices prosciutto (120g)
20g butter
1 medium brown onion (150g), chopped finely
2 cloves garlic, crushed
1 fresh long red chilli, chopped finely
1 medium red capsicum (150g), chopped coarsely
½ cup (125ml) dry white wine
½ cup (125ml) chicken stock
400g can diced tomatoes
2 tablespoons tomato paste
2 tablespoons white wine vinegar
2 anchovy fillets, chopped finely
½ cup finely chopped fresh basil
½ cup (60g) seeded black olives, halved
2 tablespoons rinsed, drained baby capers

1 Preheat oven to 200°C/180°C fan-forced.
2 Discard necks from quails. Rinse quails under cold water; pat dry inside and out with absorbent paper. Tuck legs along body; wrap tightly with prosciutto to hold legs in place.
3 Melt butter in large flameproof baking dish; cook quail, in batches, until browned.
4 Reserve 1 tablespoon quail drippings in dish; discard remainder. Heat drippings; cook onion, garlic, chilli and capsicum, stirring, until onion softens. Add wine; bring to the boil. Boil, uncovered, until liquid reduces by half. Stir in stock, undrained tomatoes, paste, vinegar, anchovy and half the basil. Return quail to dish; bring to the boil.
5 Transfer to oven; cook, turning occasionally, about 30 minutes or until quail is cooked through.
6 Remove from oven; stir in olives and capers. Divide quail among serving plates, spoon over sauce; sprinkle with remaining basil.

preparation time 15 minutes
cooking time 45 minutes **serves** 4
nutritional count per serving 24.4g total fat
(8.2g saturated fat); 1831kJ (438 cal);
10.2g carbohydrate; 38.6g protein; 2.5g fibre
note Recipe is not suitable to freeze.

tip In southern Italy and Sicily this dish is known as braciole and in the northern regions it is called involtini; our version of this classic veal dish also has a burst of sage. If you prefer to have pasta with the rolls, skip adding the potatoes.

tip For the more common version of this dish, you can use a kilo of chicken pieces instead of the quail. Cacciatore means "hunter-style", and a truly authentic recipe will call for rabbit.

creamy chickpea and garlic soup

2 cups (400g) dried chickpeas
1 tablespoon olive oil
1 large brown onion (200g), chopped coarsely
4 cloves garlic, crushed
1.75 litres (7 cups) water
2 bay leaves
1 sprig fresh rosemary
300ml cream

1 Place chickpeas in large bowl, cover with water; stand overnight, drain. Rinse under cold water, drain.
2 Heat oil in large saucepan; cook onion and garlic, stirring, until onion softens. Add chickpeas, the water, bay leaves and rosemary; bring to the boil. Reduce heat; simmer, covered, about 2 hours or until chickpeas are tender. Remove from heat; cool 5 minutes.
3 Discard bay leaves and rosemary. Using hand-held blender, process soup in pan until smooth. Add cream; stir over medium heat until hot.

preparation time 10 minutes (plus standing time)
cooking time 2 hours 20 minutes **serves** 4
nutritional count per serving 39.9g total fat (22.5g saturated fat); 2048kJ (490 cal); 21.1g carbohydrate; 10g protein; 6.9g fibre
note Recipe is suitable to freeze before adding the cream.

chicken and mushroom soup with basil pesto

¼ cup (60ml) olive oil
400g chicken breast fillets, chopped coarsely
3 green onions, sliced thinly
3 cloves garlic, crushed
300g mushrooms, sliced thinly
3 cups (750ml) chicken stock
2 cups (500ml) water
100g cauliflower, chopped coarsely
2 small potatoes (240g), chopped coarsely
½ cup (125ml) cream
¼ cup (65g) basil pesto
1 tablespoon lemon juice

1 Heat 1 tablespoon of the oil in large saucepan; cook chicken, in batches, until browned.
2 Heat remaining oil in same pan; cook onion, garlic and mushrooms, stirring, about 5 minutes or until mushrooms soften. Add stock, the water, cauliflower and potato; bring to the boil. Reduce heat; simmer, uncovered, 20 minutes. Remove from heat; cool 5 minutes.
3 Using hand-held blender, process soup in pan until smooth. Return chicken to pan with cream; stir over medium heat until hot. Serve bowls of soup drizzled with combined pesto and juice.

preparation time 15 minutes
cooking time 40 minutes **serves** 4
nutritional count per serving 37.1g total fat (13.3g saturated fat); 2140kJ (512 cal); 11.7g carbohydrate; 31.9g protein; 4.2g fibre
note Recipe is not suitable to freeze.

vegetarian three-cheese lasagne

2 cups (500ml) bottled tomato pasta sauce
3 fresh lasagne sheets (150g)
¾ cup (110g) drained semi-dried tomatoes in oil,
  chopped coarsely
100g piece fetta cheese, crumbled
½ cup (120g) firm ricotta cheese, crumbled
1½ cups (180g) coarsely grated cheddar cheese
1 cup (150g) drained marinated char-grilled
  eggplant, chopped coarsely
¾ cup (165g) drained char-grilled capsicum
125g baby rocket leaves

1 Preheat oven to 200°C/180°C fan-forced.
2 Oil deep 2.5-litre (10-cup) ovenproof dish. Spread
½ cup pasta sauce over base of dish; top with a lasagne
sheet and another ½ cup pasta sauce. Top with semi-dried
tomato, ¼ cup of each cheese, then another lasagne sheet.
Top with ½ cup pasta sauce, eggplant, remaining fetta,
remaining ricotta and another ¼ cup cheddar. Top with
remaining lasagne sheet, remaining sauce and capsicum;
sprinkle with remaining cheddar.
3 Bake, covered, 30 minutes. Uncover; bake 15 minutes.
Stand 5 minutes before cutting; serve with rocket.

preparation time 10 minutes
cooking time 45 minutes **serves** 4
nutritional count per serving 38.4g total fat
(17.2g saturated fat); 2876kJ (688 cal);
49.6g carbohydrate; 31.4g protein; 9.9g fibre
note Recipe is not suitable to freeze.

tip We don't recommend that you freeze cooked vegetables as they tend to have a spongy texture and "leftover" look about them once they've been thawed. Mushrooms, eggplant and members of the squash family are especially freezer unfriendly.

pesto-marinated chicken breasts on mediterranean vegetables

4 chicken breast fillets (800g)
2 tablespoons basil pesto
2 tablespoons olive oil
1 medium red capsicum (200g), cut into thick strips
1 medium yellow capsicum (200g), cut into thick strips
1 small red onion (100g), cut into thin wedges
1 large zucchini (150g), chopped coarsely
1 small eggplant (230g), halved, sliced thinly
¼ cup loosely packed fresh basil leaves

1 Preheat oven to 240°C/220°C fan-forced.
2 Combine chicken and pesto in medium bowl.
3 Combine oil and vegetables in large shallow baking dish. Place chicken on vegetables; roast, uncovered, about 35 minutes or until chicken is cooked and vegetables are tender.
4 Serve sprinkled with basil.

preparation time 20 minutes
cooking time 35 minutes **serves** 4
nutritional count per serving 18g total fat
(3.3g saturated fat); 1630kJ (390 cal);
6.5g carbohydrate; 48.8g protein; 3.4g fibre
note Recipe is not suitable to freeze.

chicken, spinach and ricotta bake

You need half a large barbecued chicken (450g) for this recipe.

1 tablespoon olive oil
1 large brown onion (200g), chopped finely
2 cloves garlic, crushed
10 instant lasagne sheets (200g)
1½ cups (240g) shredded barbecue chicken meat
1 cup (100g) coarsely grated pizza cheese
3 cups (750ml) bottled tomato pasta sauce
2 cups (500ml) water
50g baby spinach leaves
½ cup (120g) firm ricotta cheese, crumbled

1 Heat oil in shallow flameproof dish; cook onion and garlic, stirring, until onion softens.
2 Meanwhile, break lasagne sheets into bite-sized pieces. Sprinkle pasta pieces, chicken and half the pizza cheese into the dish.
3 Pour combined pasta sauce and the water over top of chicken mixture. Simmer, covered, about 20 minutes or until pasta is tender.
4 Meanwhile, preheat grill.
5 Sprinkle bake with spinach, ricotta and remaining pizza cheese; grill about 5 minutes or until cheese melts. Stand, covered, 10 minutes before serving.

preparation time 20 minutes
cooking time 30 minutes **serves** 4
nutritional count per serving 18.8g total fat
(7.7g saturated fat); 2195kJ (525 cal);
49.7g carbohydrate; 34.9g protein; 6.9g fibre
note Recipe is not suitable to freeze.

italian seafood stew

1 tablespoon olive oil
1 medium brown onion (150g), chopped finely
3 cloves garlic, crushed
700g bottle tomato pasta sauce
1½ cups (375ml) fish stock
½ cup (125ml) dry white wine
2 strips lemon rind
600g uncooked medium king prawns
600g firm white fish fillets
300g clams, scrubbed
12 scallops without roe (300g)
¼ cup finely shredded fresh basil
¼ cup coarsely chopped fresh flat-leaf parsley

1 Heat oil in large saucepan; cook onion and garlic, stirring, until onion softens. Add pasta sauce, stock, wine and rind; bring to the boil. Reduce heat; simmer, covered, 20 minutes.

2 Meanwhile, shell and devein prawns, leaving tails intact. Chop fish into 2cm pieces.

3 Add clams to pan; simmer, covered, 5 minutes. Discard any clams that do not open. Add prawns, fish and scallops to pan; cook, covered, stirring occasionally, about 5 minutes or until seafood just changes colour. Stir in herbs.

preparation time 20 minutes
cooking time 50 minutes **serves** 4
nutritional count per serving 9.4g total fat
(2g saturated fat); 1772kJ (424 cal);
14.5g carbohydrate; 62g protein; 4.7g fibre
note Recipe is not suitable to freeze.

tip Veal osso buco, Italian for "bone with a hole" is another name that butchers use for veal shin, usually cut into 3cm to 5cm thick slices.

osso buco

2kg veal osso buco
½ cup (75g) plain flour
2 tablespoons olive oil
100g piece pancetta, chopped finely
1 medium brown onion (150g), chopped finely
2 trimmed celery stalks (200g), chopped finely
2 medium carrots (240g), chopped finely
2 cloves garlic, crushed
2 tablespoons tomato paste
700g bottle tomato pasta sauce
1½ cups (375ml) chicken stock
½ cup (125ml) dry white wine
4 sprigs fresh lemon thyme
2 bay leaves
2 tablespoons coarsely chopped fresh basil

1 Coat veal in flour; shake off excess. Heat oil in large deep saucepan; cook veal, in batches, until browned.
2 Add pancetta, onion, celery, carrot and garlic to same pan; cook, stirring, until onion softens.
3 Add paste; cook, stirring, 1 minute. Add pasta sauce, stock, wine, thyme and bay leaves; cook, stirring 1 minute.
4 Stand veal pieces upright in pan, pushing down into sauce mixture; bring to the boil. Reduce heat; simmer, covered, 1½ hours. Uncover; simmer about 30 minutes or until veal is almost falling off the bone.
5 Discard thyme and bay leaves. Serve osso buco sprinkled with basil.
preparation time 15 minutes
cooking time 2 hours 30 minutes **serves** 6
nutritional count per serving 8.6g total fat (1.6g saturated fat); 1701kJ (407 cal); 21.2g carbohydrate; 54.5g protein; 5.4g fibre
note Recipe is suitable to freeze at the end of step 4.

lentil soup

1 tablespoon olive oil
3 rindless bacon rashers (195g), chopped coarsely
1 medium brown onion (150g), chopped finely
1 medium carrot (120g), chopped finely
1 trimmed celery stalk (100g), chopped finely
1 cup (200g) brown lentils
410g can crushed tomatoes
1 litre (4 cups) chicken stock
1 bay leaf
¼ cup coarsely chopped fresh flat-leaf parsley

1 Heat oil in large saucepan; cook bacon, onion, carrot and celery, stirring, until onion softens.
2 Add lentils, undrained tomatoes, stock and bay leaf; bring to the boil. Reduce heat; simmer, covered, 30 minutes.
3 Discard bay leaf; serve soup sprinkled with parsley.
preparation time 15 minutes
cooking time 45 minutes **serves** 4
nutritional count per serving 13.4g total fat (3.7g saturated fat); 1484kJ (355 cal); 27.8g carbohydrate; 26.1g protein; 10.1g fibre
note Recipe is suitable to freeze at the end of step 2.

These recipes, from India, China, Japan, Vietnam, Thailand and Malaysia, deliver a punchy kick. The flavours of coconut, chilli, curry and citrus are a perfect blend.

ASIAN

chicken laksa

350g fresh thin egg noodles
1 tablespoon peanut oil
⅔ cup (200g) laksa paste
2 x 400ml cans coconut milk
2 cups (500ml) chicken stock
500g chicken thigh fillets, sliced thinly
2 kaffir lime leaves, sliced thinly
1 tablespoon lime juice
2 teaspoons fish sauce
1½ cups (120g) bean sprouts
2 green onions, sliced diagonally
2 fresh small red thai chillies, sliced diagonally
¼ cup firmly packed fresh coriander leaves

1 Place noodles in medium heatproof bowl of boiling water; separate with fork, drain.
2 Heat oil in large saucepan; cook paste, stirring, until fragrant. Add coconut milk and stock; bring to the boil. Add chicken and lime leaves; simmer, uncovered, about 10 minutes or until chicken is cooked.
3 Add noodles to pan; stir until heated through. Remove pan from heat; stir in juice and sauce.
4 Serve bowls of laksa topped with remaining ingredients.
preparation time 10 minutes
cooking time 20 minutes **serves** 4
nutritional count per serving 49.1g total fat (29g saturated fat); 3779kJ (904 cal); 75.7g carbohydrate; 38.2g protein; 3.4g fibre
note Recipe is not suitable to freeze.

tip Commercial laksa pastes, generally consisting of lemon grass, chillies, galangal, shrimp paste, onions and turmeric, vary dramatically in their heat intensity so, while we call for two-thirds of a cup in this recipe, try using less of any purchased bottled pastes until you determine how hot it makes the final dish.

slow-roasted honey and soy pork neck

1 tablespoon peanut oil

1kg piece pork neck

1 large brown onion (200g), sliced thinly

2 cloves garlic, sliced thinly

4cm piece fresh ginger (20g), sliced thinly

1 cinnamon stick

2 star anise

½ cup (125ml) salt-reduced soy sauce

½ cup (125ml) chinese cooking wine

¼ cup (90g) honey

1 cup (250ml) water

450g baby buk choy, trimmed, leaves separated

1 Preheat oven to 160°C/140°C fan-forced.

2 Heat oil in large flameproof casserole dish; cook pork, turning occasionally, until browned. Remove from dish. Add onion, garlic and ginger to same dish; cook, uncovered, until onion softens. Remove from heat.

3 Stir cinnamon, star anise, sauce, cooking wine, honey and the water into onion mixture in dish. Return pork to dish, turning to coat in spice mixture. Cover dish; transfer to oven. Cook 1 hour. Uncover; cook about 1 hour or until sauce thickens slightly. Remove pork from dish. Cover pork; stand 10 minutes before slicing.

4 Add buk choy to dish; cook, stirring, about 5 minutes or until just tender. Serve pork with buk choy and sauce.

preparation time 20 minutes

cooking time 1 hour 15 minutes serves 4

nutritional count per serving 30.6g total fat (9.8g saturated fat); 2621kJ (627 cal); 5.9g carbohydrate; 76.4g protein; 2.5g fibre

note Recipe is suitable to freeze at the end of step 3.

combination fried rice

You need to cook 1⅓ cups of white long-grain rice the day before you make this dish; spread the cooled rice on a tray, cover and refrigerate overnight.

300g uncooked small king prawns

¼ cup (60ml) peanut oil

400g chicken breast fillets, sliced thinly

3 eggs, beaten lightly

4 rindless bacon rashers (260g), chopped coarsely

1 medium brown onion (150g), chopped finely

1 medium red capsicum (200g), chopped finely

2 cloves garlic, crushed

3cm piece fresh ginger (15g), grated

3 cups cooked white long-grain rice

2 tablespoons light soy sauce

¾ cup (90g) frozen peas

3 green onions, sliced thinly

1 Shell and devein prawns, leaving tails intact.

2 Heat 1 tablespoon of the oil in wok; stir-fry chicken, in batches, until cooked. Stir-fry prawns, in batches, until changed in colour.

3 Heat half the remaining oil in wok; stir-fry egg until just set then remove from wok.

4 Heat remaining oil in wok; stir-fry bacon, brown onion, capsicum, garlic and ginger until bacon is crisp. Return chicken, prawns and egg to wok with remaining ingredients; stir-fry until hot.

preparation time 25 minutes

cooking time 15 minutes serves 4

nutritional count per serving 35.1g total fat (9.4g saturated fat); 3001kJ (718 cal); 46.5g carbohydrate; 52.3g protein; 3.9g fibre

note Recipe is not suitable to freeze.

tip Thais use the whole coriander plant in their cooking to impart a stronger flavour to some dishes. This is why, when you buy a bunch of coriander at your local greengrocer, it is one of the very few fresh herbs that come with its stems and roots intact. Wash the leaves, stems and roots well before chopping them, and also scrape the roots with a small flat knife to remove some of the outer fibrous skin. After removing the leaves, finely or coarsely chop the roots and stems for use in making curry pastes or recipes like this one. Any root and stem mixture left over can be covered with peanut oil in a glass jar and stored in the refrigerator for up to two months.

thai-style beef curry

1 tablespoon peanut oil

3 large brown onions (600g), sliced thickly

2 cloves garlic, crushed

4cm piece fresh ginger (20g), grated

2 fresh long red chillies, chopped finely

1 tablespoon finely chopped
    coriander root and stem mixture

1kg gravy beef, cut into 2cm pieces

2 cups (500ml) beef stock

10cm stick fresh lemon grass (20g),
    halved lengthways, bruised

1 tablespoon tamarind concentrate

1 tablespoon grated palm sugar

2 x 400ml cans coconut milk

1 tablespoon fish sauce

800g baby new potatoes, halved

1 large red capsicum (350g), chopped coarsely

2 teaspoons lime juice

3 green onions, sliced thinly

1 cup (80g) bean sprouts

1 fresh long red chilli, sliced thinly

⅓ cup loosely packed fresh coriander leaves

1 Heat oil in large saucepan; cook brown onion, garlic, ginger, chopped chilli and coriander mixture, stirring, until onion softens.

2 Add beef, 1½ cups stock, lemon grass, tamarind, sugar, half the coconut milk and half the sauce; bring to the boil. Reduce heat; simmer, uncovered, about 1½ hours or until beef is tender.

3 Add potato, capsicum, remaining stock and remaining coconut milk; bring to the boil. Reduce heat, simmer, uncovered, about 30 minutes or until potato is tender.

4 Stir in juice, green onion and remaining sauce.

5 Serve curry sprinkled with remaining ingredients.

preparation time 20 minutes

cooking time 2 hours 15 minutes **serves** 6

nutritional count per serving 38.7g total fat
(28g saturated fat); 2809kJ (672 cal);
33.8g carbohydrate; 43.7g protein; 7.8g fibre

note Recipe is not suitable to freeze.

tip Vegetarian oyster sauce, based on mushroom extract and soybeans, has a flavour similar to oyster sauce and is often used in Asian stir-fries. Use it instead of oyster sauce in vegetarian dishes.

honey beef and noodle stir-fry

1 tablespoon sesame seeds

1 tablespoon peanut oil

800g beef strips

1 medium brown onion (150g), sliced thinly

3cm piece fresh ginger (15g), grated

1 clove garlic, crushed

1 medium red capsicum (200g), sliced thinly

115g baby corn, halved lengthways

450g hokkien noodles

⅓ cup (115g) honey

⅓ cup (80ml) teriyaki sauce

1 tablespoon mirin

1 Stir-fry sesame seeds in wok about 1 minute or until golden; remove from wok and set aside.

2 Heat half the oil in wok; stir-fry beef, in batches, until browned.

3 Heat remaining oil in wok; stir-fry onion, ginger and garlic until onion softens. Add capsicum and corn; stir-fry about 2 minutes or until capsicum is just tender.

4 Return beef to wok with noodles, honey, sauce and mirin; stir-fry until heated through.

5 Serve stir-fry sprinkled with sesame seeds.

preparation time 15 minutes

cooking time 15 minutes serves 4

nutritional count per serving 21.7g total fat (7.4g saturated fat); 3574kJ (855 cal); 101g carbohydrate; 58.9g protein; 5.3g fibre

note Recipe is not suitable to freeze.

vegetable stir-fry

1 tablespoon peanut oil

1 large brown onion (200g), sliced thinly

2 cloves garlic, crushed

450g baby buk choy, quartered lengthways

150g oyster mushrooms, halved

100g enoki mushrooms, trimmed

150g snow peas, trimmed

2 tablespoons vegetarian oyster sauce

1 fresh long red chilli, sliced thinly

¼ cup (20g) fried shallots

1 lime, cut into wedges

1 Heat oil in wok; stir-fry onion and garlic, until onion softens. Add buk choy, mushrooms and snow peas; stir-fry until just tender. Add sauce; stir-fry until heated through.

2 Serve stir-fry sprinkled with chilli and shallots, accompanied with lime.

preparation time 20 minutes

cooking time 10 minutes serves 4

nutritional count per serving 5.5g total fat (0.9g saturated fat); 506kJ (121 cal); 9.2g carbohydrate; 5.7g protein; 6.4g fibre

note Recipe is not suitable to freeze.

garlic seafood stir-fry

Buy coriander stems that have the root attached for this recipe; wash well before using.

1kg uncooked medium king prawns
500g cleaned baby squid hoods
¼ cup (60ml) peanut oil
1 tablespoon finely chopped
    coriander root and stem mixture
2 fresh small red thai chillies
½ teaspoon coarsely ground black pepper
4 cloves garlic, crushed
170g asparagus, trimmed, chopped coarsely
175g broccolini, chopped coarsely
1 cup (80g) bean sprouts
2 green onions, sliced thinly
2 tablespoons coarsely chopped fresh coriander
1 lime, cut into wedges

1 Shell and devein prawns, leaving tails intact.
2 Cut squid down centre to open out; score inside in diagonal pattern then cut into thick strips.
3 Heat half the oil in wok; cook seafood, in batches, until prawns change in colour.
4 Heat remaining oil in wok; stir-fry coriander mixture, chilli, pepper and garlic until fragrant. Add asparagus and broccolini; cook, stirring, until vegetables are almost tender. Return seafood to wok with sprouts; stir-fry until hot.
5 Serve stir-fry sprinkled with green onion and coriander, accompanied with lime.

preparation time 25 minutes
cooking time 15 minutes serves 4
nutritional count per serving 16.2g total fat
(3.1g saturated fat); 1509kJ (361 cal);
1.6g carbohydrate; 50.3g protein; 3.7g fibre
note Recipe is not suitable to freeze.

tip The duck is available from Chinese barbecued meat shops; ask the shopkeeper to chop it for you as his cleaver and experience will save you from having to do it. The duck is traditionally cooked in special ovens, and has a sweet-sticky coating made from soy sauce, chinese five-spice powder, sherry and hoisin sauce.

duck and lychee curry

⅓ cup (100g) red curry paste
⅔ cup (160ml) chicken stock
400ml can coconut milk
1 tablespoon lime juice
1 tablespoon fish sauce
2 kaffir lime leaves, shredded finely
1 whole chinese barbecued duck (1kg),
    chopped coarsely
175g broccolini, sliced lengthways
565g can lychees, rinsed, drained
225g can water chestnuts, rinsed, drained, quartered
1 fresh long red chilli, sliced thinly
¼ cup loosely packed thai basil leaves

1 Cook paste in heated large saucepan until fragrant. Add stock, coconut milk, juice, sauce and lime leaves; bring to the boil. Reduce heat; simmer, uncovered, 5 minutes.
2 Add duck, broccolini, lychees and water chestnuts to pan; bring to the boil. Reduce heat; simmer, stirring, about 5 minutes or until broccolini is tender.
3 Serve bowls of curry sprinkled with chilli and basil.

preparation time 20 minutes
cooking time 20 minutes serves 4
nutritional count per serving 66.3g total fat
(30.2g saturated fat); 3499kJ (837 cal);
23.1g carbohydrate; 35g protein; 8.2g fibre
note Recipe is not suitable to freeze.

drunken duck

1 duck (2kg)
1 tablespoon vegetable oil
1 medium brown onion (150g), chopped coarsely
2 cloves garlic, crushed
1 fresh small red thai chilli, chopped finely
4cm piece fresh ginger (20g), grated
2 cups (500ml) chinese cooking wine
1 cup (250ml) water
1 tablespoon dark soy sauce
½ teaspoon five-spice powder
15g sliced dried shiitake mushrooms
4 green onions, sliced thinly

1 Discard neck from duck. Rinse duck under cold water; pat dry inside and out with absorbent paper. Heat oil in large saucepan; cook duck until browned all over.
2 Reserve 1 tablespoon of the pan drippings; discard remainder. Heat reserved drippings in pan, add brown onion, garlic, chilli and ginger; cook, stirring, until onion softens. Return duck to pan with wine, the water, sauce, five-spice and mushrooms; bring to the boil. Reduce heat; simmer, covered, 2 hours, turning duck occasionally.
3 Carefully remove duck from pan; cut into four pieces. Divide duck among serving bowls; drizzle with pan liquid, sprinkle with green onion.

preparation time 15 minutes
cooking time 2 hours 30 minutes serves 4
nutritional count per serving 20.5g total fat
(6g saturated fat); 953kJ (22.8 cal);
1.2g carbohydrate; 7.2g protein; 0.2g fibre
note Recipe is not suitable to freeze.

barbecued pork and udon soup

1 litre (4 cups) chicken stock
2 cups (500ml) water
1 fresh small red thai chilli
10cm stick fresh lemon grass (20g),
    halved lengthways, bruised
2 tablespoons japanese soy sauce
1 teaspoon sesame oil
200g fresh udon noodles
100g fresh shiitake mushrooms, sliced thickly
230g can bamboo shoots, rinsed, drained
40g baby spinach leaves
250g chinese barbecued pork, sliced thinly

1 Combine stock, the water, chilli and lemon grass in large saucepan; bring to the boil. Reduce heat; simmer, covered, 5 minutes. Remove and discard lemon grass.
2 Add sauce, oil, noodles, mushrooms and bamboo shoots; simmer, uncovered, 5 minutes.
3 Divide spinach and pork among serving bowls; ladle hot soup into bowls.

preparation time 10 minutes
cooking time 15 minutes **serves** 4
nutritional count per serving 20.5g total fat
(8.9g saturated fat); 1735kJ (415 cal);
31.6g carbohydrate; 22.8g protein; 7.3g fibre
note Recipe is not suitable to freeze.

pumpkin and eggplant dhal

2 tablespoons olive oil
1 medium brown onion (150g), sliced thinly
2 cloves garlic, crushed
4cm piece fresh ginger (20g), grated
2 teaspoons ground cumin
2 teaspoons ground coriander
1 teaspoon ground turmeric
⅓ cup (65g) red lentils
⅓ cup (85g) yellow split peas
⅓ cup (85g) green split peas
410g can crushed tomatoes
1½ cups (375ml) vegetable stock
2 cups (500ml) water
300g piece pumpkin, chopped coarsely
1 medium eggplant (300g), chopped coarsely
400g can chickpeas, rinsed, drained

1 Heat oil in large saucepan; cook onion, garlic and ginger, stirring, until onion softens. Add spices; cook, stirring, until fragrant.
2 Add lentils and peas to pan. Stir in undrained tomatoes, stock and the water; simmer, covered, stirring occasionally, 30 minutes. Add pumpkin and eggplant; bring to the boil. Reduce heat; simmer, covered, about 20 minutes or until pumpkin is tender. Add chickpeas, simmer 10 minutes.

preparation time 15 minutes
cooking time 1 hour 15 minutes **serves** 4
nutritional count per serving 12.9g total fat
(2g saturated fat); 1793kJ (429 cal);
48.1g carbohydrate; 22.8g protein; 14.4g fibre
note Recipe is not suitable to freeze.

asian-flavoured baked mussels

1.5kg large black mussels
9cm piece fresh ginger (45g), grated
2 cloves garlic, crushed
2 kaffir lime leaves, shredded finely
2 fresh long red chillies, sliced thinly
2 medium carrots (240g), cut into matchsticks
2 medium red capsicums (400g), sliced thinly
⅓ cup (80ml) water
¼ cup (60ml) kecap manis
¼ cup (60ml) lime juice
1 cup (80g) bean sprouts
½ cup loosely packed fresh coriander leaves

1 Preheat oven to 220°C/200°C fan-forced.
2 Scrub mussels; remove beards. Combine mussels in large shallow baking dish with ginger, garlic, lime leaves, chilli, carrot, capsicum, the water, kecap manis and juice. Bake, covered, about 30 minutes or until mussels open (discard any that do not). Serve mussels sprinkled with sprouts and coriander.

preparation time 25 minutes
cooking time 30 minutes **serves** 4
nutritional count per serving 1.7g total fat (0.4g saturated fat); 502kJ (120 cal); 11.4g carbohydrate; 12.6g protein; 4.1g fibre
note Recipe is not suitable to freeze.

mango and five-spice pork spareribs

425g can mango slices, drained
2kg racks american-style pork spareribs
⅓ cup (80ml) dark soy sauce
⅓ cup (115g) honey
2 teaspoons five-spice powder
1 fresh long red chilli, chopped finely
2 cloves garlic, crushed
4cm piece fresh ginger (20g), grated

1 Preheat oven to 180°C/160°C fan-forced.
2 Blend or process mango until smooth.
3 Combine pork with mango and remaining ingredients in large shallow flameproof baking dish.
4 Cook pork, covered, 40 minutes. Remove from oven.
5 Meanwhile, preheat grill. Grill ribs, uncovered, turning and basting occasionally with pan juices, about 20 minutes or until browned.
6 Cut ribs into serving-sized pieces. Serve with steamed white rice.

preparation time 10 minutes
cooking time 1 hour **serves** 4
nutritional count per serving 8.7g total fat (3.2g saturated fat); 1739kJ (416 cal); 32.9g carbohydrate; 49.9g protein; 1.1g fibre
note Recipe is not suitable to freeze.

tip Bean thread vermicelli is called win sen in Thailand and fun si in China; while it resembles rice vermicelli in appearance, it is tougher and can be quite hard. Soak the vermicelli only long enough to soften otherwise it will become stodgy or start to fragment. This is also a good vermicelli to deep-fry to make puffed parcels.

sesame chicken stir-fry

350g bean thread vermicelli
1 tablespoon peanut oil
2 chicken breast fillets (400g), sliced thinly
1 medium brown onion (150g), sliced thinly
1 clove garlic, crushed
300g broccolini, chopped coarsely
2 tablespoons fish sauce
1 tablespoon hot chilli sauce
2 tablespoons dark soy sauce
1 tablespoon toasted sesame seeds
1 fresh long red chilli, chopped finely
4 green onions, sliced thinly
1 cup (80g) bean sprouts

1 Place vermicelli in medium heatproof bowl, cover with boiling water; stand until just tender, drain.
2 Meanwhile, heat half the oil in wok; stir-fry chicken, in batches, until browned.
3 Heat remaining oil in wok; stir-fry brown onion, garlic and broccolini until onion softens.
4 Return chicken to wok with vermicelli, combined sauces, sesame seeds and half the chilli, half the green onion and half the sprouts; stir-fry just until hot.
5 Serve stir-fry topped with remaining chilli, green onion and sprouts.

preparation time 20 minutes
cooking time 20 minutes serves 4
nutritional count per serving 9.3g total fat (1.6g saturated fat); 1325kJ (317 cal); 23.9g carbohydrate; 31.3g protein; 5.6g fibre
note Recipe is not suitable to freeze.

tip Before using a clay pot, soak it in water for about 15 minutes; this releases steam during the cooking process, which helps create a tender, flavourful dish.

tip In Indian cooking terms, masala simply means ground or blended spices (incidentally, the word has become slang for "mix" or "mixture"), so a masala can be whole spices, or a paste, or a powder. The garam masala used here is a North Indian blend of spices, and is based on varying proportions of cardamom, cloves, cinnamon, coriander, fennel and cumin, roasted and ground together. Black pepper and chilli can be added for a hotter version.

vietnamese clay pot chicken

1kg chicken thigh fillets, chopped coarsely
½ cup (125ml) chicken stock
¼ cup (60ml) lime juice
2 tablespoons fish sauce
10cm stick fresh lemon grass (20g), chopped finely
1cm piece fresh ginger (5g), grated
1 clove garlic, crushed
150g small oyster mushrooms
450g baby buk choy, chopped coarsely
4 green onions, sliced diagonally
1 fresh small red thai chilli, sliced thinly
¼ cup loosely packed fresh coriander leaves
¼ cup loosely packed vietnamese mint leaves

1 Preheat oven to 180°C/160°C fan-forced.
2 Combine chicken, stock, juice, sauce, lemon grass, ginger and garlic in 2-litre (8-cup) clay pot or ovenproof dish. Cook, covered, 30 minutes. Add mushrooms and buk choy. Cook, covered, in oven, about 30 minutes or until chicken is cooked. Serve chicken mixture topped with remaining ingredients.

preparation time 15 minutes
cooking time 1 hour **serves** 4
nutritional count per serving 18.6g total fat
(5.6g saturated fat); 1626kJ (389 cal);
3.2g carbohydrate; 50.6g protein; 4g fibre
note Recipe is not suitable to freeze.

indian dry beef curry

2 tablespoons peanut oil
2 medium brown onions (300g), chopped coarsely
4 cloves garlic, crushed
4cm piece fresh ginger (20g), grated
2 teaspoons ground cumin
2 teaspoons ground coriander
2 teaspoons ground garam masala
1 teaspoon ground turmeric
1.5kg beef chuck steak, cut into 2cm pieces
1 cup (250ml) beef stock
½ cup (140g) yogurt
¼ cup loosely packed fresh coriander leaves

1 Heat oil in large saucepan; cook onion, garlic, ginger and spices, stirring occasionally, until onion softens. Add beef; cook, stirring, until beef is covered in spice mixture.
2 Add stock to pan; bring to the boil. Reduce heat; simmer, covered, 1 hour, stirring occasionally.
3 Uncover; cook about 30 minutes or until liquid has almost evaporated and beef is tender, stirring occasionally.
4 Serve curry topped with yogurt and sprinkled coriander. Accompany with mango chutney and warm naan or steamed white rice.

preparation time 10 minutes
cooking time 1 hour 45 minutes **serves** 6
nutritional count per serving 18.3g total fat
(6.4g saturated fat); 1659kJ (397 cal);
4.5g carbohydrate; 53g protein; 1.1g fibre
note Recipe is suitable to freeze at the end of step 3.

Mediterranean cooks have always used fresh produce from the land and the sea, and enhanced it with herbs and spices to create recipes where fresh simple flavours shine through.

MEDITERRANEAN

lamb, apricot and almond tagine

2 tablespoons olive oil
1kg diced lamb
12 shallots (300g), halved
1 medium red capsicum (200g), chopped coarsely
2 cloves garlic, crushed
2cm piece fresh ginger (10g), grated
1 teaspoon ground cumin
1½ cups (375ml) water
1½ cups (375ml) chicken stock
½ teaspoon saffron threads
1 cup (150g) dried apricots halves
1 tablespoon finely chopped preserved lemon
200g green beans, trimmed, chopped coarsely
½ cup (70g) slivered almonds

1 Heat half the oil in large saucepan; cook lamb, in batches, until browned.
2 Heat remaining oil in same pan; cook shallot, capsicum, garlic, ginger and cumin, stirring, until fragrant.
3 Return lamb to pan; add the water, stock and saffron, bring to the boil. Reduce heat; simmer, covered, about 1 hour or until lamb is tender. Add apricots, lemon and beans; simmer, uncovered, 15 minutes.
4 Serve tagine sprinkled with nuts.

preparation time 20 minutes
cooking time 1 hour 30 minutes **serves** 4
nutritional count per serving 41.7g total fat (12.1g saturated fat); 3018kJ (722 cal); 22.1g carbohydrate; 61.3g protein; 7.8g fibre
note Recipe is suitable to freeze.

tip A North African specialty, whole or quartered lemons preserved in a mixture of salt, olive oil and lemon juice are added to tagines to infuse them with a rich, salty-sour flavour. A tablespoon of rinsed, finely chopped preserved lemon rind beaten into a cup of thick yogurt is excellent dolloped over a curry or stew, stirred into a salad or its dressing, or mixed into mashed potatoes or steamed rice.

tip Char-grilled capsicum is a staple of the Mediterranean kitchen, and making your own is easy; its flavoursome flesh will add an extra lift to many of your favourite recipes. Just cook the capsicum, skin-side up, under a very hot grill, or in a very hot oven, until the skin has blistered and blackened. Cover in plastic wrap or paper for 5 minutes then peel away the skin. Store the roasted, sliced flesh, covered with olive oil in a tightly sealed glass jar, in the refrigerator, taking only as much as you need for any given recipe.

spicy tomato and capsicum soup

2 teaspoons olive oil

1 medium brown onion (150g), chopped finely

½ teaspoon dried chilli flakes

1 clove garlic, crushed

410g can tomato puree

5 medium tomatoes (750g), chopped finely

1⅓ cups (285g) drained char-grilled capsicum in oil

2 medium potatoes (400g), chopped coarsely

1 litre (4 cups) chicken stock

400g can cannellini beans, rinsed, drained

1 Heat oil in large saucepan; cook onion, chilli and garlic, stirring, until onion softens. Add puree, tomato and capsicum; cook, stirring, about 1 minute or until tomato softens.

2 Add potato and half the stock to pan; bring to the boil. Reduce heat; simmer, covered, about 25 minutes or until potato is tender; cool 10 minutes.

3 Using hand-held mixer, process soup in pan until smooth. Add remaining stock and beans; stir over medium heat until hot.

preparation time 20 minutes

cooking time 30 minutes **serves** 4

nutritional count per serving 9.3g total fat (1.3g saturated fat); 1275kJ (305 cal); 35g carbohydrate; 14.9g protein; 11.6g fibre

note Recipe is not suitable to freeze.

lemon-scented cheese-filled squid

1 cup (240g) firm ricotta cheese, crumbled

200g piece fetta cheese, crumbled

150g spinach, trimmed, shredded finely

2 teaspoons finely grated lemon rind

1 tablespoon lemon juice

8 cleaned baby squid hoods (720g)

2 teaspoons olive oil

1 small brown onion (80g), chopped finely

2 cloves garlic, crushed

½ cup (125ml) dry red wine

2 x 410g cans tomato puree

2 tablespoons finely chopped fresh oregano

2 tablespoons finely chopped fresh basil

1 cinnamon stick

2 bay leaves

⅓ cup (40g) seeded black olives

600g baby new potatoes, halved

1 Combine ricotta, half the fetta, spinach, rind and juice in small bowl.

2 Fill squid with cheese mixture; seal ends with toothpicks.

3 Heat oil in large saucepan; cook onion and garlic, stirring, until onion softens. Add wine, puree, fresh herbs, cinnamon and bay leaves; bring to the boil. Reduce heat; simmer, covered, 30 minutes.

4 Add squid, olives and potato to pan; simmer, covered, 15 minutes or until potato is just tender. Serve sprinkled with remaining fetta.

preparation time 25 minutes

cooking time 45 minutes **serves** 4

nutritional count per serving 23.5g total fat (13g saturated fat); 2525kJ (604 cal); 35.1g carbohydrate; 53.2g protein; 8.6g fibre

note Recipe is not suitable to freeze.

tip With a name that loosely translates as "top of the shop", ras el hanout is a Moroccan blend of the very best spice that a spice merchant has to offer: allspice, cumin, paprika, fennel, caraway and saffron are all generally part of the mix.

moroccan beef couscous

2 tablespoons olive oil
4 x 220g new-york cut steaks
1 tablespoon ras el hanout
1 tablespoon finely grated lemon rind
⅓ cup (80ml) lemon juice
⅔ cup (160ml) dry white wine
1 cup (250ml) water
1 small red onion (100g), chopped finely
2 cups (400g) couscous
¼ cup coarsely chopped fresh flat-leaf parsley
½ cup coarsely chopped fresh mint
¼ cup (50g) toasted pepitas
⅓ cup (95g) yogurt

1 Heat oil in large deep frying pan; rub beef with ras el hanout. Cook beef, uncovered, until cooked as desired, turning once only. Remove from pan; stand, covered, 5 minutes.
2 Meanwhile, add rind, juice, wine and the water to same cleaned pan; cover, bring to the boil then remove from heat. Add onion and couscous; cover, stand about 5 minutes or until liquid is absorbed, fluffing with fork occasionally. Stir in herbs and pepitas.
3 Serve couscous topped with sliced steak and yogurt.
preparation time 10 minutes
cooking time 10 minutes serves 4
nutritional count per serving 29.6g total fat (8.5g saturated fat); 3687kJ (882 cal); 82.3g carbohydrate; 64.3g protein; 2.5g fibre
note Recipe is not suitable to freeze.

tip Swiss brown mushrooms, also known as roman or cremini, are light-to-dark-brown in colour with a full bodied flavour. Store on a tray in a single layer, covered with dampened absorbent paper, in a spot where cool air can circulate freely around them.

chicken, chilli and tomato stew

2 tablespoons olive oil
1kg chicken thigh fillets, chopped coarsely
1 medium brown onion (150g), chopped finely
3 cloves garlic, crushed
½ teaspoon ground cumin
2 x 410g cans chopped tomatoes
1 cup (250ml) chicken stock
1 tablespoon coarsely chopped fresh oregano
¼ cup (60g) drained sliced jalapeño chillies
420g can kidney beans, rinsed, drained

1 Heat half the oil in large deep frying pan; cook chicken, in batches, until browned.
2 Heat remaining oil in same pan; cook onion and garlic, stirring, until onion softens. Add cumin; cook, stirring, until fragrant.
3 Return chicken to pan with undrained tomatoes and stock; bring to the boil. Reduce heat; simmer, covered, about 25 minutes or until sauce thickens slightly.
4 Add oregano, chillies and beans; stir until mixture is heated through.

preparation time 15 minutes
cooking time 30 minutes **serves** 4
nutritional count per serving 28.3g total fat
(7g saturated fat); 2345kJ (561 cal);
19g carbohydrate; 54.1g protein; 8.1g fibre
note Recipe is not suitable to freeze.

chicken and asparagus pilaf

40g butter
400g chicken breast fillets, chopped coarsely
1 medium red onion (170g), chopped finely
3 cloves garlic, crushed
200g swiss brown mushrooms, chopped coarsely
1½ cups (300g) basmati rice
¾ cup (180ml) dry white wine
1½ cups (375ml) chicken stock
2 teaspoons finely grated lemon rind
1 tablespoon lemon juice
2¼ cups (560ml) water
170g asparagus, trimmed, chopped coarsely
100g green beans, trimmed, chopped coarsely
1 tablespoon fresh thyme leaves
2 tablespoons roasted pine nuts

1 Heat half the butter in large saucepan; cook chicken, in batches, until cooked through.
2 Heat remaining butter in same pan; cook onion and garlic, stirring, until onion softens. Add mushrooms; cook, stirring, until just tender.
3 Add rice to pan; cook, stirring, 1 minute. Add wine; cook, stirring, until liquid is absorbed.
4 Add stock, rind, juice and 2 cups of the water to pan; bring to the boil. Reduce heat; simmer, uncovered, stirring occasionally, about 20 minutes or until liquid is absorbed and rice is just tender.
5 Stir chicken, asparagus, beans, thyme and remaining water into pilaf; cook, covered, over low heat, about 5 minutes or until vegetables are tender and chicken is hot. Serve pilaf sprinkled with nuts.

preparation time 20 minutes
cooking time 1 hour **serves** 4
nutritional count per serving 16.6g total fat
(6.6g saturated fat); 2433kJ (582 cal);
64.3g carbohydrate; 33.5g protein; 4.3g fibre
note Recipe is not suitable to freeze.

braised veal shoulder with white beans

¼ cup (60ml) olive oil

1.2kg boned veal shoulder, rolled, tied

2 medium brown onions (300g), sliced thickly

3 cloves garlic, crushed

½ cup (125ml) dry red wine

1 cinnamon stick

2 bay leaves

2 sprigs rosemary

2 x 410g cans crushed tomatoes

½ cup (60g) seeded green olives

2 medium carrots (240g), chopped coarsely

½ cup (60g) frozen peas

400g can white beans, rinsed, drained

1 Preheat oven to 200°C/180°C fan-forced.

2 Heat 2 tablespoons of the oil in large flameproof dish; cook veal, turning frequently, until browned.

3 Heat remaining oil in same dish; cook onion and garlic, stirring, until onion softens. Add wine, cinnamon, bay leaves, rosemary, undrained tomatoes and olives; bring to the boil.

4 Return veal to dish; cover. Transfer to oven; cook, 30 minutes. Turn veal and stir tomato mixture. Add carrots; cook, covered, 30 minutes.

5 Remove veal from dish; cover to keep warm. Add peas and beans to dish; cook, covered, 10 minutes.

6 Serve roasted vegetables with sliced veal.

preparation time 10 minutes

cooking time 1 hour 30 minutes **serves** 6

nutritional count per serving 14.7g total fat (2.8g saturated fat); 1697kJ (406 cal); 12.7g carbohydrate; 49.2g protein; 5.4g fibre

note Recipe is not suitable to freeze.

saganaki prawns

1 tablespoon olive oil

1 medium white onion (150g), chopped finely

4 cloves garlic, crushed

410g can crushed tomatoes

¾ cup (180ml) dry white wine

2kg uncooked medium king prawns

¼ cup coarsely chopped fresh flat-leaf parsley

¼ cup coarsely chopped fresh oregano

200g piece fetta cheese, crumbled

1 Heat oil in large frying pan; cook onion and garlic, stirring, until onion softens. Add undrained tomatoes and wine; bring to the boil. Reduce heat; simmer, covered, 10 minutes, stirring occasionally.

2 Meanwhile, shell and devein prawns, leaving tails intact.

3 Add prawns and herbs to tomato mixture; simmer, covered, 10 minutes, stirring occasionally.

4 Meanwhile, preheat grill.

5 Sprinkle cheese over prawn mixture; grill, uncovered, until cheese browns lightly.

preparation time 15 minutes

cooking time 30 minutes **serves** 4

nutritional count per serving 18g total fat (8.6g saturated fat); 1956kJ (468 cal); 5.8g carbohydrate; 61.8g protein; 2.4g fibre

note Recipe is not suitable to freeze.

tip Ask your butcher to bone, roll and tie the meat for you. Many varieties of white beans are available canned, among them great northern, navy, cannellini, butter and haricot beans; any of these is suitable for this recipe. Drain beans then rinse well under cold water before using them.

tip Saganaki, despite sounding vaguely Japanese, is the traditional Greek name for a snack or entrée of grilled or fried cheese (fetta, kasseri, haloumi or kefalograviera), which is then sprinkled with lemon juice and eaten with bread. It has evolved, however, into a descriptive culinary term for any dish that uses cooked cheese as one of the main ingredients, such as the saganaki prawns found here and on many restaurant menus.

tip You need a medium frying pan having a heatproof handle and a 20cm base for this recipe. If the pan handle is not heatproof, wrap it tightly in a few layers of foil; place the pan under the grill, but keep the handle away from the heat, if possible.

tomato, basil and pancetta omelette

1 tablespoon olive oil
1 small red onion (100g), sliced thinly
1 clove garlic, crushed
4 slices pancetta (60g), chopped coarsely
1 small tomato (90g), sliced thinly
8 eggs, beaten lightly
1 cup (100g) packaged breadcrumbs
⅓ cup finely chopped fresh basil
½ cup loosely packed fresh basil leaves
1 teaspoon balsamic vinegar

1 Preheat grill.
2 Heat half the oil in medium frying pan; cook onion, garlic and pancetta, stirring, until onion softens. Arrange tomato slices over pancetta mixture.
3 Carefully pour combined egg, breadcrumbs and chopped basil into pan; cook, over low heat, until omelette is almost set.
4 Place pan under grill until omelette sets and top is browned lightly.
5 Carefully turn omelette, bottom-side up, onto serving plate, sprinkle with basil leaves; drizzle with combined remaining oil and vinegar.

preparation time 15 minutes
cooking time 20 minutes **serves** 4
nutritional count per serving 16.9g total fat (4.4g saturated fat); 1300kJ (311 cal); 18.7g carbohydrate; 20.2g protein; 2g fibre
note Recipe is not suitable to freeze.

pork belly and chorizo stew

2 chorizo (340g), sliced thinly
600g piece pork belly, rind removed, cut into 3cm pieces
1 large brown onion (200g), sliced thinly
2 cloves garlic, crushed
1 teaspoon sweet smoked paprika
1 large red capsicum (350g), chopped coarsely
800g can chopped tomatoes
½ cup (125ml) dry red wine
½ cup (125ml) water
400g can white beans, rinsed, drained
½ cup finely chopped fresh flat-leaf parsley

1 Cook chorizo and pork, stirring, in batches, in large flameproof casserole dish until browned. Add onion and garlic to dish; cook, stirring, until onion softens.
2 Return meats to dish with paprika, capsicum, undrained tomatoes, wine and the water; bring to the boil. Reduce heat; simmer, covered, 40 minutes. Add beans; simmer, uncovered, about 20 minutes or until pork is tender and sauce thickens slightly. Serve stew sprinkled with parsley.

preparation time 25 minutes
cooking time 1 hour 10 minutes **serves** 4
nutritional count per serving 55g total fat (19.1g saturated fat); 3331kJ (797 cal); 26.7g carbohydrate; 47g protein; 7.9g fibre
note Recipe is not suitable to freeze.

mediterranean baked fish

4 whole white fish (1.2kg)
2 tablespoons finely chopped fresh basil
2 tablespoons finely chopped fresh flat-leaf parsley
2 tablespoons finely chopped fresh oregano
2 tablespoons olive oil
4 cloves garlic, crushed
2 medium lemons (280g), sliced thinly
½ cup (125ml) dry white wine
4 medium tomatoes (600g), chopped coarsely

1 Preheat oven to 200°C/180°C fan-forced.
2 Place fish in large ovenproof dish. Combine herbs, half the oil and half the garlic in small jug; spread 1 tablespoon of herb mixture into each fish cavity. Rub fish with remaining oil, then cover with lemon slices.
3 Stir remaining garlic, wine and tomato into dish; cook, uncovered, about 30 minutes or until fish is cooked through.
preparation time 15 minutes
cooking time 30 minutes **serves** 4
nutritional count per serving 12.7g total fat
(2.6g saturated fat); 1112kJ (266 cal);
4.7g carbohydrate; 26g protein; 4.5g fibre
note Recipe is not suitable to freeze.

lamb with warm kumara and chickpea salad

8 french-trimmed lamb shanks (2kg)
1 tablespoon finely grated lemon rind
¼ cup (60ml) lemon juice
3 cloves garlic, crushed
2 tablespoons sumac
½ cup (125ml) dry white wine
½ cup (125ml) chicken stock
2 medium kumara (800g), cut into 2cm pieces
2 medium brown onions (300g), sliced thinly
150g baby spinach leaves
¼ cup (35g) coarsely chopped
    roasted unsalted pistachios
300g can chickpeas, rinsed, drained

1 Preheat oven to 180°C/160°C fan-forced.
2 Place lamb in large ovenproof dish. Combine rind, juice, garlic and sumac in small jug; rub mixture over lamb. Add wine and stock to dish; cook, uncovered, 2 hours, turning halfway through cooking.
3 Add kumara and onion to dish; cook, covered, about 40 minutes or until lamb is tender.
4 Using slotted spoon, place kumara mixture in large serving bowl; add remaining ingredients, stir gently. Serve lamb with salad.
preparation time 15 minutes
cooking time 2 hours 40 minutes **serves** 4
nutritional count per serving 21.3g total fat
(7.7g saturated fat); 2700kJ (646 cal);
36g carbohydrate; 67.8g protein; 8.3g fibre
note Recipe is not suitable to freeze.

tip We used snapper in this recipe, but you can use any white firm-fleshed fish you like.

tip French green lentils, also known as puy lentils, were originally grown in the town of Puy in France. They are tiny, green-blue lentils with a nutty, earthy flavour and a hardy nature, which allows them to be rapidly cooked without disintegrating.

harira

½ cup (100g) french green lentils
500g diced lamb, cut into 1cm pieces
1 medium brown onion (150g), chopped finely
2 cloves garlic, crushed
½ teaspoon ground cinnamon
½ teaspoon ground ginger
½ teaspoon hot paprika
1 teaspoon ground turmeric
pinch saffron threads
1.5 litres (6 cups) water
400g can chickpeas, rinsed, drained
½ cup (100g) white long-grain rice
3 small egg tomatoes (180g), chopped finely
¼ cup finely chopped fresh flat-leaf parsley

1 Cook lentils, lamb, onion, garlic and spices in large flameproof casserole dish, stirring, until lamb is browned. Add the water; bring to the boil. Reduce heat; simmer, covered, 1 hour.

2 Add chickpeas, rice and tomato to dish; simmer, uncovered, about 20 minutes or until rice is just tender. Stir in parsley.

preparation time 20 minutes

cooking time 1 hour 20 minutes **serves** 4

nutritional count per serving 13.1g total fat (5.3g saturated fat); 1919kJ (459 cal); 41.4g carbohydrate; 39.1g protein; 8.3g fibre

note Recipe is not suitable to freeze.

harissa and mint vegetable stew

40g butter
10 shallots (250g), halved
6 cloves garlic, crushed
2 tablespoons plain flour
2 cups (500ml) vegetable stock
2 cups (500ml) water
1kg baby new potatoes, halved
410g can crushed tomatoes
2 tablespoons harissa paste
1 cinnamon stick
½ cup firmly packed fresh mint leaves
500g yellow patty-pan squash, halved
115g baby corn
½ cup (60g) frozen peas
250g cherry tomatoes, halved

1 Heat butter in large saucepan; cook shallot and garlic, stirring, until shallot softens. Add flour; cook, stirring, 1 minute.

2 Add stock, the water, potato, undrained tomatoes, harissa, cinnamon and about two-thirds of the mint leaves to pan; bring to the boil. Reduce heat; simmer, uncovered, 30 minutes.

3 Add squash to pan; simmer, uncovered, 20 minutes. Add corn, peas and cherry tomato; simmer, uncovered, 10 minutes. Serve stew sprinkled with remaining mint.

preparation time 15 minutes

cooking time 1 hour 15 minutes **serves** 4

nutritional count per serving 10.3g total fat (5.7g saturated fat); 1705kJ (408 cal); 55.7g carbohydrate; 15.7g protein; 14.3g fibre

note Recipe is not suitable to freeze.

chicken and fig tagine

1 tablespoon olive oil

1kg chicken thigh fillets, chopped coarsely

1 medium red onion (170g), chopped finely

1 trimmed celery stalk (100g), chopped coarsely

2 cloves garlic, crushed

1 teaspoon ground cumin

1 teaspoon ground coriander

1 teaspoon ground ginger

1 teaspoon ground cinnamon

1 teaspoon ground turmeric

2 cups (500ml) chicken stock

¾ cup (150g) dried figs, sliced thickly

1 medium red capsicum (200g), chopped coarsely

1 teaspoon finely grated lemon rind

¼ cup coarsely chopped fresh coriander

¼ cup (35g) coarsely chopped
roasted unsalted pistachios

1 Heat oil in large saucepan; cook chicken, in batches, until browned.

2 Add onion, celery, garlic and spices to same pan; cook, stirring, until onion softens.

3 Return chicken to pan; stir to coat in spice mixture. Add stock; bring to the boil. Reduce heat; simmer, covered, about 30 minutes or until chicken is almost cooked.

4 Add fig, capsicum and rind to pan; simmer, uncovered, about 15 minutes or until sauce thickens slightly.

5 Stir in fresh coriander; serve tagine sprinkled with nuts.

preparation time 20 minutes

cooking time 1 hour **serves** 4

nutritional count per serving 27.9g total fat
(7g saturated fat); 2441kJ (584 cal);
27.2g carbohydrate; 52.6g protein; 8g fibre

note Recipe is suitable to freeze at the end of step 3.

beef and bean casserole

2 tablespoons olive oil

1kg beef chuck steak, cut into 2cm pieces

2 medium brown onions (300g), chopped finely

2 cloves garlic, crushed

1 teaspoon ground turmeric

2 teaspoons ground cumin

½ teaspoon dried chilli flakes

¼ cup (70g) tomato paste

410g can crushed tomatoes

2 cups (500ml) beef stock

2 bay leaves

2 medium potatoes (400g), chopped coarsely

400g can kidney beans, rinsed, drained

¼ cup coarsely chopped fresh coriander

¼ cup coarsely chopped fresh flat-leaf parsley

1 Heat oil in large saucepan; cook beef, in batches, until browned.

2 Add onion and garlic to pan; cook, stirring, until onion softens. Add spices; cook, stirring, until fragrant. Add paste; cook, stirring, 1 minute.

3 Return beef to pan with undrained tomatoes, stock and bay leaves; bring to the boil. Reduce heat; simmer, covered, 1 hour.

4 Add potato to pan; simmer, uncovered, about 30 minutes or until potato is tender.

5 Discard bay leaves. Add beans to pan; stir until heated through. Remove from heat, stir through herbs.

preparation time 20 minutes

cooking time 2 hours **serves** 4

nutritional count per serving 21.4g total fat
(6.2g saturated fat); 2383kJ (570 cal);
28.8g carbohydrate; 60.8g protein; 8.9g fibre

note Recipe is suitable to freeze at the end of step 3.

Finish off your one-pot meal with a delicious one-pot dessert. These tarts and puddings, pies and slices are simple, and scrumptious, as the end of the meal should be.

SWEET THINGS

baked apples with butterscotch sauce

6 medium apples (900g)
50g butter, cut into 12 cubes
¼ cup (55g) brown sugar
⅓ cup (40g) finely chopped pecans
1 tablespoon brown sugar, extra
⅓ cup (80ml) cream

1 Preheat oven to 180°C/160°C fan-forced.
2 Core unpeeled apples about three-quarters of the way down from stem end, making hole 4cm in diameter. Use small sharp knife to score around centre of each apple. Stand apples upright in small ovenproof dish.
3 Place one cube of butter and a teaspoon of brown sugar in cavity of each apple; pack nuts firmly into apple cavity. Divide remaining butter and sugar among apples; sprinkle extra sugar around apples.
4 Bake 45 minutes. Stir cream into dish; bake about 10 minutes. Transfer apples to serving bowls. Whisk cream in dish briefly; drizzle over apples.

preparation time 10 minutes
cooking time 55 minutes **serves** 6
nutritional count per serving 17.5g total fat (8.6g saturated fat); 1145kJ (274 cal); 26.7g carbohydrate; 1.3g protein; 3g fibre
note Recipe is not suitable to freeze.

tip We used Golden Delicious apples for this recipe; they are a crisp almost citrus-coloured apple with an excellent flavour and good keeping properties. It's probably the best cooking apple around, but you can substitute it with green-skinned Granny Smiths, another good cooking apple.

choc-mint self-saucing pudding

60g butter

½ cup (125ml) milk

2 tablespoons cocoa powder

1 cup (150g) self-raising flour

¾ cup (165g) caster sugar

100g mint-flavoured dark eating chocolate,
  chopped coarsely

¾ cup (165g) firmly packed brown sugar

2 cups (500ml) boiling water

1 Preheat oven to 180°C/160°C fan-forced. Grease 1.5-litre (6-cup) ovenproof dish.

2 Heat butter and milk in ovenproof dish in microwave oven on HIGH (100%) for 20 seconds or until butter melts.

3 Stir half the sifted cocoa, sifted flour, caster sugar and chocolate into butter mixture. Sift remaining cocoa and brown sugar over mixture; pour the boiling water gently over mixture.

4 Bake about 40 minutes or until centre is firm. Stand 5 minutes before serving.

preparation time 10 minutes

cooking time 40 minutes **serves** 4

nutritional count per serving 21.6g total fat (13.5g saturated fat); 3064kJ (733 cal); 125.8g carbohydrate; 6.9g protein; 1.9g fibre

note Recipe is not suitable to freeze.

date and apricot creamy rice

1 litre (4 cups) milk

⅔ cup (150g) caster sugar

1 cinnamon stick

2 teaspoons finely grated lemon rind

½ cup (100g) uncooked arborio rice

½ cup (75g) coarsely chopped dried apricots

½ cup (115g) coarsely chopped fresh dates

¼ cup (35g) coarsely chopped
  roasted unsalted pistachios

1 Combine milk, sugar, cinnamon and rind in medium saucepan; bring to the boil. Gradually stir rice into boiling milk mixture. Reduce heat; simmer, covered, stirring occasionally, about 1 hour or until rice is tender and liquid is almost absorbed.

2 Discard cinnamon stick; stir in apricots and dates, sprinkle with nuts.

preparation time 10 minutes

cooking time 1 hour **serves** 6

nutritional count per serving 9.6g total fat (4.6g saturated fat); 1480kJ (354 cal); 56.5g carbohydrate; 8.6g protein; 2.4g fibre

note Recipe is not suitable to freeze.

one pot sweet things

tip This dessert is called "impossible" because, while a runny mixture is poured into the cake pan, a three-layered "pie" emerges from the oven. The bottom layer is pastry-like because the flour and butter sink to the bottom; the centre layer is like a custard filling; and the top layer is slightly browned and crusty because the coconut, the lightest ingredient, floats to the top during baking.

blueberry impossible pie

½ cup (75g) plain flour
1 cup (220g) caster sugar
1 cup (80g) desiccated coconut
4 eggs, beaten lightly
1 teaspoon vanilla extract
125g butter, melted
2 cups (500ml) milk
½ cup (75g) fresh or frozen blueberries

1 Preheat oven to 180°C/160°C fan-forced. Grease deep 24cm pie dish.
2 Combine sifted flour, sugar, coconut, egg, vanilla, butter and milk in dish; sprinkle with berries.
3 Bake about 45 minutes or until browned lightly and just set. Stand 10 minutes before serving.
preparation time 10 minutes
cooking time 1 hour **serves** 8
nutritional count per serving 24.5g total fat (16.6g saturated fat); 1710kJ (409 cal); 39.2g carbohydrate; 7.2g protein; 2g fibre
note Recipe is not suitable to freeze.

florentine slice

¾ cup (120g) sultanas
2 cups (80g) corn flakes
¾ cup (110g) unsalted peanuts
1 cup (175g) coarsely chopped milk eating chocolate
½ cup (100g) red glacé cherries, halved
395g can sweetened condensed milk
¼ cup (60ml) Ice Magic chocolate topping

1 Preheat oven to 180°C/160°C fan-forced. Grease base of 20cm x 30cm lamington pan; line base with baking paper, extending paper 5cm over long sides.
2 Combine sultanas, corn flakes, nuts, chocolate and cherries in pan; drizzle condensed milk all over mixture.
3 Bake, uncovered, about 15 minutes or until browned lightly; cool in pan. Drizzle slice with chocolate topping; refrigerate until set. Cut into small rectangles to serve.
preparation time 10 minutes
cooking time 15 minutes **makes** 24
nutritional count per piece 5.1g total fat (2.1g saturated fat); 598kJ (143 cal); 20.4g carbohydrate; 3.3g protein; 0.7g fibre
note Recipe is not suitable to freeze.

peach and walnut galettes

1 sheet ready-rolled puff pastry
20g butter, melted
¼ cup (55g) raw sugar
⅓ cup (40g) finely chopped walnuts
4 canned peach halves in natural juice, drained

1 Preheat oven to 180°C/160°C fan-forced. Grease oven tray; line with baking paper.
2 Cut pastry into quarters; place quarters on tray, prick pastry with fork, brush with butter.
3 Divide sugar and nuts among pastry squares, leaving 1cm border around each.
4 Slice peach halves thinly; divide among pastry squares. Bake about 10 minutes or until pastry is golden brown.
preparation time 5 minutes
cooking time 10 minutes **makes** 4
nutritional count per galette 20.5g total fat (8.2g saturated fat); 1451kJ (347 cal); 35.9g carbohydrate; 4.1g protein; 2g fibre

hazelnut tiramisu

3 teaspoons instant coffee granules
⅓ cup (75g) caster sugar
1 cup (250ml) boiling water
⅓ cup (80ml) hazelnut-flavoured liqueur
300ml cream
1 cup (250g) mascarpone cheese
250g packet sponge-finger biscuits
½ cup (70g) coarsely chopped roasted hazelnuts
½ cup (90g) finely chopped milk eating chocolate

1 Dissolve coffee and half the sugar in the boiling water in medium heatproof jug. Stir in liqueur; cool.
2 Combine cream, cheese and remaining sugar in medium bowl; stir until smooth.
3 Place biscuits, in single layer, in shallow 1.5-litre (6-cup) baking dish. Pour coffee mixture evenly over biscuits; sprinkle with half the nuts then half the chocolate. Spread cream mixture carefully over top then sprinkle with remaining nuts and chocolate. Cover; refrigerate overnight.
preparation time 15 minutes (plus refrigeration time)
serves 8
nutritional count per serving 40.9g total fat (23.4g saturated fat); 2437kJ (583 cal); 42.3g carbohydrate; 7.2g protein; 1.6g fibre
note Recipe is not suitable to freeze.

white chocolate and macadamia parcels

4 sheets fillo pastry
20g butter, melted
1 cup (240g) soft ricotta cheese
2 teaspoons caster sugar
¼ cup (35g) coarsely chopped roasted unsalted macadamias
½ cup (90g) coarsely chopped white eating chocolate
2 tablespoons honey

1 Preheat oven to 180°C/160°C fan-forced. Grease oven tray; line with baking paper.
2 Cut one pastry sheet in half crossways; brush one half with butter, place unbuttered half on top. Repeat process with remaining sheets. You will have four pastry stacks.
3 Centre a quarter of the cheese on each pastry stack then sprinkle each with a quarter of the combined sugar, nuts and chocolate. Fold ends of pastry towards the centre; roll from one side to enclose filling. Place parcels, seam-side down, on tray.
4 Bake about 10 minutes or until pastry is golden brown. Serve parcels drizzled with honey.
preparation time 10 minutes
cooking time 10 minutes **makes** 4
nutritional count per parcel 25.3g total fat (12.7g saturated fat); 1701kJ (407 cal); 34.8g carbohydrate; 10g protein; 0.7g fibre
note Recipe is not suitable to freeze.

tip Sponge-finger biscuits, also known as Savoiardi, are from the Piedmont region of Italy. They are the traditional sponge-finger cake-like biscuits used in making a tiramisu, but they're also used in making other semifreddi and charlottes. Be certain the ones you buy are crisp; if soft, they're past their use-by date. They are available from supermarkets.

tip Sponge-finger biscuits are also known as Savoiardi, Savoy biscuits, lady's fingers or sponge fingers; they are long, oval-shaped Italian-style crisp fingers made from sponge-cake mixture, and are available from supermarkets.

apricot and strawberry sponge bake

250g packet sponge-finger biscuits
1¼ cups (300g) sour cream
250g strawberries, sliced thinly
820g can apricot halves in natural juice, drained
⅓ cup (75g) firmly packed brown sugar
2 tablespoons coarsely chopped fresh mint

1 Preheat oven to 220°C/200°C fan-forced.
2 Place biscuits, in single layer, in 2.5-litre (10-cup) ovenproof dish. Spread sour cream over biscuits; top with fruit then sprinkle with sugar.
3 Bake about 15 minutes. Stand 5 minutes before serving sprinkled with mint.

preparation time 10 minutes
cooking time 15 minutes **serves** 8
nutritional count per serving 16.3g total fat (10.2g saturated fat); 1279kJ (309 cal); 34.8g carbohydrate; 4.7g protein; 2.5g fibre
note Recipe is not suitable to freeze.

apple, raspberry and almond bake

2 medium apples (300g), peeled, cored,
   cut into fine dice
2 cups (300g) frozen raspberries
½ cup (110g) firmly packed brown sugar
2 tablespoons lemon juice
¼ cup (30g) almond meal
⅓ cup (30g) rolled oats
⅓ cup (20g) flaked almonds

1 Preheat oven to 180°C/160°C fan-forced. Grease 1.5-litre (6-cup) ovenproof dish.
2 Combine apple, berries, half the sugar, juice and almond meal in dish. Sprinkle with oats, remaining brown sugar and nuts.
3 Bake about 25 minutes or until browned lightly.

preparation time 5 minutes
cooking time 25 minutes **serves** 6
nutritional count per serving 5.3g total fat (0.4g saturated fat); 782kJ (187 cal); 29.4g carbohydrate; 3g protein; 4.6g fibre
note Recipe is not suitable to freeze.

caramel fondue with fresh fruit

½ cup (110g) firmly packed brown sugar
⅔ cup (160ml) cream
50g butter
250g strawberries, halved
2 medium bananas (400g), sliced thickly
2 small pears (360g), sliced thinly

1 Combine sugar, cream and butter in small saucepan. Cook, stirring, until sugar dissolves and butter melts; bring to the boil. Reduce heat; simmer, uncovered, 3 minutes.
2 Remove from heat; cool 10 minutes before serving with fruit.
preparation time 5 minutes
cooking time 5 minutes **serves** 4
nutritional count per serving 27.7g total fat (18.2g saturated fat); 2002kJ (479 cal); 52.8g carbohydrate; 3.3g protein; 4.6g fibre
note This recipes makes 1 cup (250ml) sauce. The sauce is suitable to freeze.

choc-peanut bombes

300ml thickened cream
100g dark eating chocolate, melted
¼ cup (35g) coarsely chopped unsalted peanuts
2 x 60g Snickers bars, chopped finely

1 Beat cream in small bowl with electric mixer until soft peaks form; add cooled chocolate, beat until combined. Fold in remaining ingredients; refrigerate 2 hours.
preparation time 5 minutes (plus refrigeration time)
serves 4
nutritional count per serving 46.8g total fat (27.5g saturated fat); 2475kJ (592 cal); 35g carbohydrate; 7.5g protein; 3.1g fibre
note Recipe is not suitable to freeze.

one pot sweet things

tip Caramel Top'n'Fill is a caramel filling made from milk and cane sugar that can be used straight from the can for slices, tarts and cheesecakes.

tip Made from vanilla bean extract, vanilla bean seeds, sugar and natural thickeners, vanilla bean paste can be used as a substitute for a whole vanilla bean or vanilla extract. It is available from the baking section of major supermarkets.

banoffee tart

1 sheet ready-rolled sweet shortcrust pastry
380g can Caramel Top 'n' Fill
2 medium bananas (400g), sliced thinly
300ml double cream
½ teaspoon ground nutmeg

1 Preheat oven to 200°C/180°C fan-forced. Grease 24cm-round loose-based fluted flan tin.
2 Ease pastry into tin; press into base and side. Trim edge; prick base all over with fork. Cover; refrigerate 10 minutes.
3 Place tin on oven tray. Line pastry case with baking paper; fill with dried beans or rice. Bake 15 minutes; remove paper and beans carefully from pie shell. Bake 10 minutes; cool. Fill with caramel; refrigerate overnight.
4 Top caramel with banana, then spread with cream. Serve sprinkled with nutmeg.

preparation time 5 minutes (plus refrigeration time)
cooking time 25 minutes **serves** 8
nutritional count per serving 28.7g total fat
(18.2g saturated fat); 1839kJ (440 cal);
39.7g carbohydrate; 5.6g protein; 1.1g fibre
note Recipe is not suitable to freeze.

caramelised pears

4 medium pears (920g)
40g butter
½ cup (110g) firmly packed brown sugar
2 tablespoons coffee-flavoured liqueur
½ teaspoon vanilla bean paste
1 litre vanilla ice-cream

1 Peel and core pears; cut each pear into eight wedges.
2 Melt butter in large frying pan, add pear; cook, stirring occasionally, until softened slightly.
3 Sprinkle sugar over pear, reduce heat. Cook, stirring occasionally, until sugar dissolves. Bring to the boil; boil 1 minute. Add liqueur and paste; cook, over high heat, about 2 minutes or until mixture is syrupy.
4 Serve pear with ice-cream; drizzle with syrup.

preparation time 10 minutes
cooking time 15 minutes **serves** 4
nutritional count per serving 24.9g total fat
(16.1g saturated fat); 2470kJ (591 cal);
81.4g carbohydrate; 5.8g protein; 3.4g fibre
note Recipe is not suitable to freeze.

roasted rhubarb and cranberries

1kg rhubarb, trimmed, chopped coarsely
¼ cup (35g) dried cranberries
¼ cup (55g) brown sugar
1 tablespoon orange juice

1 Preheat oven to 180°C/160°C fan-forced.
2 Combine ingredients in medium shallow baking dish. Roast, uncovered, about 20 minutes or until rhubarb is just tender.
3 Serve rhubarb topped with orange-flavoured mascarpone (see serving suggestion, right).

preparation time 5 minutes
cooking time 20 minutes **serves** 4
nutritional count per serving 0.6g total fat (0g saturated fat); 568kJ (136 cal); 24.2g carbohydrate; 4g protein; 8.4g fibre
note Recipe is not suitable to freeze.

dark chocolate, raspberry and brioche pudding

40g butter, softened
300g brioche, sliced thickly
¼ cup (80g) raspberry jam
¾ cup (135g) coarsely grated dark eating chocolate
3 eggs
¼ cup (55g) caster sugar
2½ cups (625ml) milk, heated
½ cup (75g) frozen raspberries

1 Preheat oven to 180°C/160°C fan-forced. Grease shallow 2-litre (8-cup) ovenproof dish.
2 Butter one side of each brioche slice; spread unbuttered side with jam, sprinkle with chocolate.
3 Arrange brioche, butter-side up, overlapping slightly, in dish.
4 Whisk eggs, sugar and milk in large jug; pour over brioche, sprinkle with raspberries and any remaining chocolate.
5 Place dish in large baking dish; add enough boiling water to come halfway up side of dish.
6 Bake about 55 minutes or until pudding sets. Remove pudding from baking dish; stand 5 minutes before serving.

preparation time 15 minutes
cooking time 55 minutes **serves** 6
nutritional count per serving 24.6g total fat (13.6g saturated fat); 2186kJ (523 cal); 62g carbohydrate; 12.4g protein; 2.1g fibre
note Recipe is not suitable to freeze.

serving suggestion Combine
1 cup mascarpone cheese,
2 teaspoons finely grated orange
rind, 2 teaspoons orange juice,
2 teaspoons orange-flavoured
liqueur and 1 tablespoon sifted
icing sugar in a small bowl. Dollop
onto warm roasted rhubarb.

tip Heating the milk before
adding it to the pudding
reduces its cooking time.

tip Vanilla bean paste is made from vanilla pods and contains real seeds. It is highly concentrated and 1 teaspoon replaces a whole vanilla pod without mess or fuss, as you neither have to split or scrape the pod. It can also be used instead of vanilla extract. It is found in most supermarkets in the baking section.

tip You can use any combination of dried fruit in this recipe and, if you prefer, you can serve the compote warm with vanilla ice-cream rather than cream.

orange-poached pears

6 medium pears (1.4kg)
2 cups (500ml) water
2 cups (500ml) dry red wine
2 tablespoons orange-flavoured liqueur
¾ cup (165g) caster sugar
1 teaspoon vanilla bean paste
4 x 5cm strips orange rind
⅓ cup (80ml) orange juice

1 Peel pears, leaving stems intact.
2 Combine the remaining ingredients in large saucepan; stir over heat, without boiling, until sugar dissolves. Add pears; bring to the boil. Reduce heat; simmer, covered, about 1 hour or until pears are tender.
3 Transfer pears to serving bowls. Bring syrup in pan to the boil. Boil, uncovered, about 10 minutes or until syrup thickens slightly. Serve pears drizzled with warm syrup.

preparation time 5 minutes
cooking time 1 hour 15 minutes **serves** 6
nutritional count per serving 0.2g total fat (0g saturated fat); 1317kJ (315 cal); 57.1g carbohydrate; 0.8g protein; 3.5g fibre
note Recipe is not suitable to freeze.

spiced fruit compote

1 cup (250ml) water
1 cup (250ml) dry white wine
½ cup (110g) caster sugar
4 x 2.5cm strips orange rind
1 teaspoon vanilla bean paste
2 cinnamon sticks
3 cardamom pods, bruised
1 cup (150g) dried apricot halves
8 dried figs (120g), halved
⅔ cup (100g) dried mango
4 fresh dates (60g), halved, seeded
½ cup (70g) dried cranberries
½ cup (125ml) cream
¼ teaspoon ground cinnamon

1 Combine the water, wine, sugar, rind, paste, cinnamon and cardamom in medium saucepan. Stir, over low heat, until sugar dissolves; bring to the boil. Reduce heat; simmer, uncovered, without stirring, 15 minutes.
2 Add fruit; simmer, uncovered, stirring occasionally, about 15 minutes or until fruit softens. Cool fruit in syrup.
3 Serve compote topped with cream and sprinkled with ground cinnamon.

preparation time 15 minutes (plus cooling time)
cooking time 40 minutes **serves** 4
nutritional count per serving 14.2g total fat (9g saturated fat); 2433kJ (582 cal); 92.1g carbohydrate; 5.2g protein; 11g fibre
note Recipe is not suitable to freeze.

GLOSSARY

ALMONDS flat, pointy-tipped nuts having a pitted brown shell enclosing a creamy white kernel that is covered by a brown skin.
flaked paper-thin slices.
slivered small pieces cut lengthways.

BAMBOO SHOOTS the tender shoots of bamboo plants. Available in cans; must be rinsed and drained before use.

BLUE SWIMMER CRAB also known as sand crab, blue manna crab, bluey or sandy. Substitute with lobster, balmain or moreton bay bugs.

BEANS
borlotti also known as roman beans or pink beans; available as fresh or dried. Interchangeable with pinto beans because of the similarity in appearance – both are pale pink or beige with dark red streaks.
broad also known as fava, windsor and horse beans; available dried, fresh, canned and frozen. Fresh and frozen forms should be peeled twice (discarding both the outer long green pod and the beige-green tough inner shell).
white in this book, some recipes may simply call for "white beans", a generic term we use for canned or dried cannellini, haricot, navy or great northern beans.

BREADCRUMBS
fresh bread is processed into crumbs.
packaged prepared fine-textured, but crunchy, white breadcrumbs.
stale crumbs made by blending or processing one- or two-day-old bread.

BREADS
brioche French in origin; a rich, yeast-leavened, cake-like bread made with butter and eggs. Most common form is the brioche à tête, a round fluted roll topped with a much smaller ball of dough. Available from cake or specialty bread shops.
mountain bread wrap a soft-textured thin, dry bread that is most often filled then rolled up before eating. Available from supermarkets and health-food stores.

BROCCOLINI a cross between broccoli and chinese kale; long asparagus-like stems with a long loose floret, both completely edible. Resembles broccoli in look but is milder and sweeter in taste.

BUK CHOY also known as bok choy, pak choi, chinese white cabbage or chinese chard; has a fresh, mild mustard taste. Use both stems and leaves. Baby buk choy, also known as pak kat farang or shanghai bok choy, is much smaller and more tender than buk choy.

BUTTER use salted or unsalted (sweet) butter; 125g is equal to one stick (4 ounces) of butter.

CAPSICUM native to central and South America. Also known as bell pepper or, simply, pepper; found in red, green, yellow, orange or purplish-black varieties. Discard seeds and membranes before use.

CHEESE
fetta Greek in origin; a crumbly textured goats- or sheep-milk cheese having a sharp, salty taste.
mascarpone an Italian fresh cultured-cream product made in much the same way as yogurt. White to creamy yellow in colour, with a buttery-rich, luscious texture.
parmesan also known as parmigiana; a hard, grainy cows-milk cheese. The curd is salted in brine for a month before being aged for up to two years.
pizza a blend of varying proportions of processed grated mozzarella, cheddar and parmesan cheeses.
ricotta a sweet, moist, white cows-milk cheese with a slightly grainy texture. The name roughly translates as "cooked again" and refers to ricotta's manufacture from a whey that is itself a by-product of other cheese making.
swiss generic name for a variety of slightly firm to hard swiss cheeses, among them emmentaler and gruyère.

CHICKPEAS also called channa, hummus or garbanzos; an irregularly round, sandy-coloured legume. Retains a firm texture even after cooking; has a floury mouth-feel and robust nutty flavour. Is available canned or dried (the latter need to soak for several hours in cold water before being used).

CHILLI always use rubber gloves when seeding and chopping fresh chillies as they can burn your skin. We use unseeded chillies in our recipes because the seeds contain the heat; use fewer chillies rather than seeding the lot. Whole chillies freeze well; wrap two or three chillies in plastic and keep in the freezer until required. Chillies can also be hung and dried.
cayenne also known as cayenne pepper; a thin-fleshed, long, extremely hot, dried red chilli, usually purchased ground.
jalapeño pronounced hah-lah-pain-yo. Fairly hot, medium-sized, plump, dark green chilli; available pickled, sold canned or bottled, and fresh, from greengrocers.
long red available both fresh and dried; a generic term used for any moderately hot, long, thin chilli (about 6cm to 8cm long).

powder the Asian variety is the hottest, made from dried ground thai chillies. Can be used instead of fresh chillies in the proportion of ½ teaspoon chilli powder to 1 medium chopped fresh red chilli.
thai also known as "scuds"; tiny, very hot and bright red in colour.

CHINESE COOKING WINE also known as shao hsing or chinese rice wine; made from fermented rice, wheat, sugar and salt with a 13.5 per cent alcohol content. Found in Asian food shops; if you can't find it, use mirin or sherry, instead.

CHOCOLATE
dark eating also known as semi-sweet or luxury chocolate; made of a high percentage of cocoa liquor and cocoa butter, and a little added sugar. Unless stated otherwise, we use dark eating chocolate in this book.
Ice Magic a chocolate flavouring that sets within seconds after being poured over cold desserts such as ice-cream.
milk eating most popular eating chocolate, mild and very sweet; similar in make-up to dark chocolate with the difference being the addition of milk solids.
mint-flavoured dark eating any dark eating chocolate flavoured with mint essences.
white eating contains no cocoa solids but derives its sweet flavour from cocoa butter.

CORIANDER also known as pak chee, cilantro or chinese parsley; bright-green leafy herb with a pungent flavour. Both the stems and roots of coriander are also used in Thai cooking; wash well before using. Coriander seeds are also available but are no substitute for fresh coriander, as the taste is very different.

CURLY ENDIVE also known as frisée; a prickly-looking, curly-leafed green vegetable having an edible white heart. Fairly bitter in flavour, like chicory, with which it is often confused.

DRIED CRANBERRIES have the same slightly sour, succulent flavour as fresh cranberries. Available in most supermarkets.

FENNEL also known as finocchio or anise; a roundish, crunchy, pale green-white vegetable. The bulb has a slightly sweet, anise flavour but the leaves have a much stronger taste. Also sometimes the name given to the dried seeds of the plant, which have a stronger licorice flavour.

FILLO PASTRY (also fillo or phyllo); delicate tissue-thin pastry sheets purchased chilled or frozen. It is best brushed with butter or margarine before baking.

FLOUR

cornflour also known as cornstarch; used as a thickening agent in cooking.

plain an all-purpose wheat flour.

self-raising plain flour sifted with baking powder in the proportion of 1 cup flour to 2 teaspoons baking powder.

FRIED GARLIC (kratiem jiew) sprinkled over cooked dishes. Can be purchased canned or in cellophane bags at Asian grocery stores; once opened, will keep for months if tightly sealed. Make your own by thinly slicing garlic and shallow-frying in vegetable oil until golden brown and crisp.

FRIED SHALLOT (homm jiew) sprinkled over cooked dishes. Can be purchased canned or in cellophane bags at Asian grocery stores; once opened, will keep for months if tightly sealed. Make your own by thinly slicing shallots or baby onions and shallow-frying in vegetable oil until golden brown and crisp.

GARAM MASALA a blend of spices based on cardamom, cinnamon, cloves, fennel, coriander and cumin, roasted and ground together. Black pepper and chilli can be added for a hotter version.

GINGER, FRESH also known as green or root ginger; the thick gnarled root of a tropical plant.

HORSERADISH CREAM a commercially prepared creamy paste made of grated horseradish, vinegar, oil and sugar.

KAFFIR LIME LEAVES also known as bai magrood; look like two glossy dark green leaves joined end to end, forming a rounded hourglass shape. Sold fresh, dried or frozen, the dried leaves are less potent so double the number if using them as a substitute for fresh; a strip of fresh lime peel may be substituted for each kaffir lime leaf.

KALAMATA OLIVES small, sharp-tasting, brine-cured black olives.

KIPFLER POTATOES small, finger-shaped potato having a nutty flavour.

LEMON GRASS a tall, clumping, lemon-smelling and tasting, sharp-edged aromatic tropical grass; the white lower part of the stem is used, finely chopped.

LIQUEURS

coffee-flavoured we used either Kahlua or Tia Maria.

hazelnut-flavoured we used Frangelico.

orange-flavoured we used Grand Marnier or Cointreau.

LYCHEES a small fruit from China with a hard shell and sweet, juicy flesh. The white flesh has a gelatinous texture and musky, perfumed taste. Discard the rough skin and seed before using. Also available canned in a sugar syrup.

MIRIN a Japanese champagne-coloured cooking wine; made of glutinous rice and alcohol and used expressly for cooking. Should not be confused with sake. Also available is a seasoned sweet mirin called manjo mirin made of water, rice, corn syrup and alcohol.

MUSHROOMS

button small, cultivated white mushrooms with a mild flavour. When a recipe in this book calls for an unspecified type of mushroom, use button.

enoki clumps of long, spaghetti-like stems with tiny, snowy-white caps.

oyster also known as abalone; grey-white mushrooms shaped like a fan with virtually no stalk. Prized for their smooth texture and subtle, oyster-like flavour.

shiitake when fresh are also known as forest, chinese black or golden oak mushrooms; although cultivated, they have the earthiness and taste of wild mushrooms. Are large and meaty. When dried, are known as donko or dried chinese mushrooms; rehydrate before use.

swiss brown also known as roman or cremini. Light to dark brown mushrooms with a full-bodied flavour.

MUSTARD

dijon a pale brown, distinctively flavoured, fairly mild french mustard.

wholegrain also known as seeded mustard. A french-style coarse-grain mustard made from dijon-style mustard and crushed mustard seeds.

NESTLÉ TOP 'N' FILL CARAMEL a delicious filling made from milk and cane sugar. Has similar qualities to sweetened condensed milk, only a thicker, caramel consistency, which is great to use in caramel desserts.

NEW-YORK CUT boneless striploin beef.

NOODLES

bean thread vermicelli also known as wun sen, made from mung bean paste; also known as cellophane or glass noodles because they are transparent when cooked. White in colour (not off-white like rice vermicelli), very delicate and fine. Must be soaked to soften before use; using them deep-fried requires no pre-soaking.

fresh egg also known as ba mee or yellow noodles; made from wheat flour and eggs. Range in size from very fine strands to wide, spaghetti-like pieces as thick as a shoelace. Also sold dried.

hokkien also known as stir-fry noodles; fresh wheat noodles resembling thick, yellow-brown spaghetti needing no pre-cooking before use.

rice vermicelli also known as sen mee, mei fun or bee hoon. Similar to bean thread noodles, only longer and made with rice flour instead of mung bean starch. Before using, soak in hot water until softened, boil briefly then rinse with hot water.

udon available fresh and dried; these broad, white, wheat Japanese noodles are similar to the ones in home-made chicken noodle soup.

OIL

olive made from ripened olives. Extra virgin and virgin are the first and second press, respectively, and are considered the best; the extra light or light name on other types refers to taste, not fat levels.

peanut pressed from ground peanuts; the most commonly used oil in Asian cooking because of its capacity to handle high heat without burning (high smoke point).

vegetable sourced from plants.

ONIONS

brown and white are interchangeable. Their pungent flesh adds flavour to a vast range of dishes.

green also known as scallion or, incorrectly, shallot; an immature onion picked before the bulb has formed, having a long, bright-green edible stalk.

red also known as spanish, red spanish or bermuda onion; a sweet-flavoured, large, purple-red onion.

shallots also called french shallots, golden shallots or eschalots; small, brown-skinned, elongated members of the onion family. Grows in tight clusters similar to garlic.

spring have small white bulbs and long, narrow green-leafed tops.

PANCETTA an Italian unsmoked bacon, cured in salt and spices then rolled into a sausage shape and dried for several weeks.

PASTES

harissa a Moroccan sauce or paste made from dried chillies, cumin, garlic, oil and caraway seeds; harissa can be used as a rub for meats, a sauce and dressing ingredient, or as a condiment eaten on its own. It is available in supermarkets and Middle Eastern grocery stores.

laksa a bottled paste containing galangal, lemon grass, chillies, shrimp paste, onions and turmeric.

red curry a very popular curry paste; is a medium-hot blend of chilli, garlic, onion, lemon grass, spice, galangal and salt.

PEARL BARLEY has had the husk removed then been hulled and polished so that only the "pearl" of the original grain remains, much the same as white rice.

PORK BELLY a lower-cost cut of meat due to the relatively high traces of fat in it. However, this means that the cuts are ideal for longer cooking periods and recipes where the meat might dry out.

PRESERVED LEMON RIND a North African specialty; lemons are quartered and preserved in salt and lemon juice. To use, remove and discard pulp, squeeze juice from rind, rinse rind well then slice thinly.

PROSCIUTTO a kind of unsmoked Italian ham; salted, air-cured and aged, it is usually eaten uncooked.

RAS EL HANOUT is a classic spice blend used in Moroccan cooking. Meaning "top of the shop" this is the very best spice blend that a spice merchant has to offer.

RICE

arborio small, round-grain rice, well-suited to absorb a large amount of liquid; especially suitable for risottos.

basmati a white, fragrant, long-grained rice. Wash several times before cooking.

long-grain an elongated grain that remains separate when cooked; the most popular steaming rice in Asia.

medium-grain previously sold as calrose rice; an extremely versatile rice that can be substituted for short- or long-grain rice, if necessary.

SAFFRON THREADS available in strands or ground form; imparts a yellow-orange colour to food once infused. Should be stored in the freezer.

SALT unless specified otherwise, we use normal iodised table salt. Because we believe cooks salt as they like or not at all; the vast majority of our recipes do not list it as one of the ingredients.

SAUCES

fish also known as nam pla or nuoc nam; made from pulverised salted fermented fish (most often anchovies). Has a pungent smell and strong taste. There are many versions of varying intensity, so use according to your taste.

hot chilli we use a hot Chinese variety made from red thai chillies, salt and vinegar. Use sparingly, increasing the quantity to suit your taste.

kecap manis a dark, thick sweet soy sauce. The sweetness is derived from the addition of either molasses or palm sugar when brewed.

soy made from fermented soy beans. Several variations are available in most supermarkets and Asian food stores.

dark soy deep brown, almost black in colour; rich, with a thicker consistency than other types. Pungent but not particularly salty, it is good for marinating.

japanese soy an all-purpose low-sodium soy sauce made with more wheat content than its Chinese counterparts. Possibly the best table soy and the one to choose if you only want one variety.

light soy a pale, fairly thin, but salty tasting sauce; used in dishes in which the natural colour of the ingredients is to be maintained. Not to be confused with salt-reduced or low-sodium soy sauces.

teriyaki a Japanese sauce made from soy sauce, mirin, sugar, ginger and other spices.

sweet chilli a thin, mild sauce made from red chillies, sugar, garlic and vinegar.

tomato also known as ketchup or catsup; made from tomatoes, vinegar and spices.

vegetarian mushroom oyster a "vegetarian" oyster sauce made from blended mushrooms and soy sauce.

worcestershire a dark coloured sauce made from garlic, soy sauce, tamarind, onions, molasses, lime, anchovies, vinegar and seasonings. Available in supermarkets.

SPATCHCOCK a small chicken (poussin), no more than 6 weeks old, weighing a maximum 500g. Also, a cooking technique where a small chicken is split open, then flattened and grilled.

SPONGE-FINGER BISCUITS also known as Savoiardi, Savoy biscuits or lady's fingers; are long, oval-shaped Italian-style crisp fingers made from sponge-cake mixture.

SUGAR

brown an extremely soft, finely granulated sugar retaining molasses for its characteristic colour and flavour.

caster also known as superfine or finely granulated table sugar.

palm also known as nam tan pip, jaggery, jawa or gula melaka; made from the sap of the sugar palm tree. Light brown to black in colour and usually sold in rock-hard cakes. Substitute with brown sugar, if unavailable.

white a coarse, granulated table sugar, also known as crystal sugar.

SUMAC a purple-red, astringent spice ground from berries growing on shrubs that flourish wild around the Mediterranean; adds a tart, lemony flavour.

TAMARIND CONCENTRATE the distillation of tamarind juice into a condensed, compacted paste. Thick and purple-black, it requires no soaking or straining; adds a sweet-sour, slightly astringent taste.

VANILLA

bean dried, long thin pod from a tropical golden orchid; the minuscule black seeds inside the bean impart a luscious vanilla flavour. Place a whole bean in a jar of sugar to make the vanilla sugar often called for in recipes; a bean can be used three or four times before losing its flavour.

bean paste made from vanilla bean extract, vanilla bean seeds, sugar and natural thickeners. Can be used as a substitute for vanilla beans.

extract obtained from vanilla beans infused in water; a non-alcoholic version of essence.

VINEGAR

balsamic made from the juice of Trebbiano grapes; is a deep rich brown colour with a sweet and sour flavour. There are now many balsamic vinegars on the market ranging in pungency and quality depending on how long they have been aged. Quality can be determined up to a point by price; use the most expensive sparingly.

brown made from fermented malt and beech shavings.

sherry made from a blend of wines and left in wood vats to mature where they develop a rich mellow flavour.

white wine made from white wine.

WATER CHESTNUTS resembles a chestnut in appearance, hence the English name. They are small brown tubers with a crisp, white, nutty-tasting flesh. Their crunchy texture is best experienced fresh, however, canned water chestnuts are more easily obtained and can be kept about a month, once opened, under refrigeration.

WOMBOK also known as chinese cabbage, peking or napa cabbage; elongated in shape with pale green, crinkly leaves, this is the most common cabbage in South-East Asia.

ZUCCHINI also known as courgette; a small, pale- or dark-green, yellow or white vegetable belonging to the squash family.

MEASURES

One Australian metric measuring cup holds approximately 250ml; one Australian metric tablespoon holds 20ml; one Australian metric teaspoon holds 5ml.

The difference between one country's measuring cups and another's is within a two- or three-teaspoon variance, and will not affect your cooking results. North America, New Zealand and the United Kingdom use a 15ml tablespoon.

All cup and spoon measurements are level. The most accurate way of measuring dry ingredients is to weigh them. When measuring liquids, use a clear glass or plastic jug with the metric markings.

We use large eggs with an average weight of 60g.

DRY MEASURES

METRIC	IMPERIAL
15g	½oz
30g	1oz
60g	2oz
90g	3oz
125g	4oz (¼lb)
155g	5oz
185g	6oz
220g	7oz
250g	8oz (½lb)
280g	9oz
315g	10oz
345g	11oz
375g	12oz (¾lb)
410g	13oz
440g	14oz
470g	15oz
500g	16oz (1lb)
750g	24oz (1½lb)
1kg	32oz (2lb)

LIQUID MEASURES

METRIC	IMPERIAL
30ml	1 fluid oz
60ml	2 fluid oz
100ml	3 fluid oz
125ml	4 fluid oz
150ml	5 fluid oz (¼ pint/1 gill)
190ml	6 fluid oz
250ml	8 fluid oz
300ml	10 fluid oz (½ pint)
500ml	16 fluid oz
600ml	20 fluid oz (1 pint)
1000ml (1 litre)	1¾ pints

LENGTH MEASURES

METRIC	IMPERIAL
3mm	⅛in
6mm	¼in
1cm	½in
2cm	¾in
2.5cm	1in
5cm	2in
6cm	2½in
8cm	3in
10cm	4in
13cm	5in
15cm	6in
18cm	7in
20cm	8in
23cm	9in
25cm	10in
28cm	11in
30cm	12in (1ft)

OVEN TEMPERATURES

These oven temperatures are only a guide for conventional ovens.
For fan-forced ovens, check the manufacturer's manual.

	°C (CELSIUS)	°F (FAHRENHEIT)	GAS MARK
Very slow	120	250	½
Slow	150	275-300	1-2
Moderately slow	160	325	3
Moderate	180	350-375	4-5
Moderately hot	200	400	6
Hot	220	425-450	7-8
Very hot	240	475	9

INDEX

ARE YOU MISSING SOME COOKBOOKS?

The Australian Women's Weekly Cookbooks are available from bookshops, cookshops, supermarkets and other stores all over the world. You can also buy direct from the publisher, using the order form below.

TITLE	RRP	QTY
100 Fast Fillets	£6.99	
A Taste of Chocolate	£6.99	
After Work Fast	£6.99	
Beginners Cooking Class	£6.99	
Beginners Simple Meals	£6.99	
Beginners Thai	£6.99	
Best Food Fast	£6.99	
Breads & Muffins	£6.99	
Brunches, Lunches & Treats	£6.99	
Cafe Classics	£6.99	
Cafe Favourites	£6.99	
Cakes Bakes & Desserts	£6.99	
Cakes Biscuits & Slices	£6.99	
Cakes Cooking Class	£6.99	
Caribbean Cooking	£6.99	
Casseroles	£6.99	
Casseroles & Slow-Cooked Classics	£6.99	
Cheap Eats	£6.99	
Cheesecakes: baked and chilled	£6.99	
Chicken	£6.99	
Chinese and the foods of Thailand, Vietnam, Malaysia & Japan	£6.99	
Chinese Cooking Class	£6.99	
Chocs & Treats	£6.99	
Cookies & Biscuits	£6.99	
Cooking Class Cake Decorating	£6.99	
Cupcakes & Fairycakes	£6.99	
Detox	£6.99	
Dinner Lamb	£6.99	
Dinner Seafood	£6.99	
Easy Comfort Food	£6.99	
Easy Curry	£6.99	
Easy Midweek Meals	£6.99	
Easy Spanish-Style	£6.99	
Food for Fit and Healthy Kids	£6.99	
Foods of the Mediterranean	£6.99	
Foods That Fight Back	£6.99	
Fresh Food Fast	£6.99	
Fresh Food for Babies & Toddlers	£6.99	
Good Food for Babies & Toddlers	£6.99	
Great Kids' Cakes (May 08)	£6.99	
Greek Cooking Class	£6.99	
Grills	£6.99	
Healthy Heart Cookbook	£6.99	
Indian Cooking Class	£6.99	
Japanese Cooking Class	£6.99	

TITLE	RRP	QTY
Just For One	£6.99	
Just For Two	£6.99	
Kids' Birthday Cakes	£6.99	
Kids Cooking	£6.99	
Kids' Cooking Step-by-Step	£6.99	
Low-carb, Low-fat	£6.99	
Low-fat Food for Life	£6.99	
Low-fat Meals in Minutes	£6.99	
Main Course Salads	£6.99	
Mexican	£6.99	
Middle Eastern Cooking Class	£6.99	
Midweek Meals in Minutes	£6.99	
Mince in Minutes	£6.99	
Moroccan & the Foods of North Africa	£6.99	
Muffins, Scones & Breads	£6.99	
New Casseroles	£6.99	
New Curries	£6.99	
New French Food	£6.99	
New Salads	£6.99	
One Pot	£6.99	
Party Food and Drink	£6.99	
Pasta Meals in Minutes	£6.99	
Quick & Simple Cooking	£6.99	
Rice & Risotto	£6.99	
Saucery	£6.99	
Sauces Salsas & Dressings	£6.99	
Sensational Stir-Fries	£6.99	
Simple Healthy Meals	£6.99	
Simple Starters Mains & Puds	£6.99	
Slim	£6.99	
Soup	£6.99	
Stir-fry	£6.99	
Superfoods for Exam Success	£6.99	
Tapas Mezze Antipasto & other bites	£6.99	
Thai Cooking Class	£6.99	
Traditional Italian	£6.99	
Vegetarian Meals in Minutes	£6.99	
Vegie Food	£6.99	
Wicked Sweet Indulgences	£6.99	
Wok Meals in Minutes	£6.99	
TOTAL COST	£	

Mr/Mrs/Ms _____

Address_____ Postcode_____

Day time phone _____email* (optional) _____

I enclose my cheque/money order for £ _____

or please charge £ _____

to my: ☐ Access ☐ Mastercard ☐ Visa ☐ Diners Club

Card number | | | | | | | | | | | | | | | | | | |

Expiry date _____ 3 digit security code *(found on reverse of card)* _____

Cardholder's name_____ Signature _____

To order: Mail or fax – photocopy or complete the order form above, and send your credit card details or cheque payable to: Australian Consolidated Press (UK), ACP Books, 10 Scirocco Close, Moulton Park Office Village, Northampton NN3 6AP. phone (+44) (0)1604 642200 fax (+44) (0)1604 642300 email books@acpuk.com or order online at www.acpuk.com

Non-UK residents: We accept the credit cards listed on the coupon, or cheques, drafts or International Money Orders payable in sterling and drawn on a UK bank. Credit card charges are at the exchange rate current at the time of payment. **Postage and packing UK:** Add £1.00 per order plus £1.75 per book. **Postage and packing overseas:** Add £2.00 per order plus £3.50 per book. All pricing current at time of going to press and subject to change/availability. **Offer ends 31.12.2008**

* By including your email address, you consent to receipt of any email regarding this magazine, and other emails which inform you of ACP's other publications, products, services and events, and to promote third party goods and services you may be interested in.

TEST KITCHEN
Food director Pamela Clark
Associate food editor Alexandra Somerville
Home economists Liz Macri, Louise Patniotis,
Angela Muscat, Rebecca Squadrito
Nutritional information Belinda Farlow

ACP BOOKS
General manager Christine Whiston
Editorial director Susan Tomnay
Creative director Hieu Chi Nguyen
Designer Hannah Blackmore
Senior editor Wendy Bryant
Director of sales Brian Cearnes
Marketing manager Bridget Cody
Business analyst Ashley Davies
Operations manager David Scotto
International rights enquiries Laura Bamford
lbamford@acpuk.com

ACP Books are published by ACP Magazines
a division of PBL Media Pty Limited
Group publisher, Women's lifestyle Pat Ingram
Director of sales, Women's lifestyle Lynette Phillips
Commercial manager, Women's lifestyle Seymour Cohen
Marketing director, Women's lifestyle Matthew Dominello
Public relations manager, Women's lifestyle Hannah Deveraux
Creative director, Events, Women's lifestyle Luke Bonnano
Research Director, Women's lifestyle Justin Stone
ACP Magazines, Chief Executive officer Scott Lorson
PBL Media, Chief Executive officer Ian Law

Produced by ACP Books, Sydney.
Published by ACP Books, a division of ACP Magazines Ltd,
54 Park St, Sydney; GPO Box 4088, Sydney, NSW 2001.
phone (02) 9282 8618 fax (02) 9267 9438.
acpbooks@acpmagazines.com.au www.acpbooks.com.au
Printed by Dai Nippon in Korea.

Australia Distributed by Network Services,
phone +61 2 9282 8777 fax +61 2 9264 3278
networkweb@networkservicescompany.com.au
United Kingdom Distributed by
Australian Consolidated Press (UK),
phone (01604) 642 200 fax (01604) 642 300
books@acpuk.com
New Zealand Distributed by Netlink
Distribution Company,
phone (9) 366 9966 ask@ndc.co.nz
South Africa Distributed by PSD Promotions,
phone (27 11) 392 6065/6/7
fax (27 11) 392 6079/80
orders@psdprom.co.za
Canada Distributed by Publishers Group Canada
phone (800) 663 5714 fax (800) 565 3770
service@raincoast.com

A catalogue record for this book is available from the British Library.
ISBN 978 186396 793 8 (pbk.)
© ACP Magazines Ltd 2008
ABN 18 053 273 546

The publishers would like to thank the following
for props used in photography: Le Creuset;
Le Chasseur; Staub (contact Trade Point);
Cote Bastide (contact Studio Imports).
Send recipe enquiries to:
askpamela@acpmagazines.com.au